EATALY

ALL ABOUT

DOLCI

TRENTINO—ALTO ADIGE
strudel di mele

LOMBARDIA
panettone

VALLE D'AOSTA
monte bianco

VENETO
tiramisù

PIEMONTE
torta di nocciole

FRIULI—VENEZIA GUILIA
gubana

EMILIA—ROMAGNA
zuppa inglese

LIGURIA
torta pinolata

LE MARCHE
ciambellone

UMBRIA
brustengo

TOSCANA
cantucci

ABRUZZO
soffioni

LAZIO
budino di ricotta

MOLISE
bocconotti

PUGLIA
cartellate

CAMPANIA
babà al rum

SARDEGNA
pardulas

BASILICATA
calzoncelli

CALABRIA
pitta 'mpigliata

SICILIA
cannoli

EATALY

ALL ABOUT
DOLCI

Regional Italian Desserts and Sweet Traditions

WRITTEN WITH NATALIE DANFORD
PHOTOGRAPHS BY FRANCESCO SAPIENZA

RIZZOLI
NEW YORK

New York · Paris · London · Milan

CONTENTS

BISCOTTI

Italian cookies add a sweet,
wholesome twist to the day.

GRANELLATI

PEARL-SUGAR COOKIES

Makes 9 to 10 dozen cookies

Pearl sugar, sometimes labeled nib sugar, consists of large chunks that do not dissolve, giving cookies like these a satisfying crunch.

4 large eggs

1 egg yolk

1¼ cups (250 grams) granulated sugar

½ teaspoon (3 grams) honey

2⅔ cups (275 grams) pastry flour

3 tablespoons (25 grams) bread flour

⅓ cup (50 grams) potato starch

1⅓ cups (250 grams) pearl sugar

PREHEAT the oven to 350°F (180°C). Line baking sheets or jelly-roll pans with parchment paper and set aside.

IN a stand mixer fitted with the whisk attachment, beat the eggs, yolk, granulated sugar, and honey until thick and light in color. Sift in the flours and potato starch and fold in with a spatula.

TRANSFER the mixture to a pastry bag fitted with a smooth tip (#4) and pipe 3-inch (7- to 8-centimeter) strips onto the prepared pans. They will spread slightly, but not too much, so you can fit a lot on each pan. Sprinkle the cookies with the pearl sugar until heavily coated and bake in the preheated oven until light golden brown and firm, 10 to 15 minutes.

CONSIGLI PER BISCOTTI COOKIE BAKING TIPS

Because most ovens have "hot spots," it is always a good idea to switch cookie sheets front-to-back and top-to-bottom about halfway through baking.

Most cookies brown underneath first. Gently lift a cookie with a spatula to check the bottom for color.

Most cookies cool on the pan on a rack briefly, then are moved directly to the rack to finish cooling. Very delicate cookies may cool completely on the pan.

You can reuse parchment paper for several batches of cookies.

OCCHI DI BUE

JAM-FILLED SANDWICH COOKIES

Makes 4 to 5 dozen sandwich cookies

Occhi di bue are bull's-eyes, a reference to the target-like appearance of these cookies. (We use the same phrase for fried eggs in Italian.) Most often these are filled with apricot jam, but you can use any flavor you like, or dab chocolate-hazelnut spread between the halves instead.

2 sticks plus 2 tablespoons (250 grams) unsalted butter, softened

1 cup (200 grams) sugar

5 egg yolks

4¾ cups (500 grams) pastry flour

Finely grated zest of 1 lemon

½ teaspoon (5 grams) salt

Confectioners' sugar for sprinkling

About 1½ cups (480 grams) jam

BEAT the butter with the sugar until well combined. Add the egg yolks and beat until combined. Gradually beat in the flour, lemon zest, and salt. Wrap the dough in plastic wrap and refrigerate until firm, 2 to 3 hours.

WHEN you are ready to bake the cookies, preheat the oven to 325°F (160°C). Line baking sheets or jelly-roll pans with parchment paper and set aside.

PLACE about one third of the dough on a lightly floured surface (leave the rest refrigerated) and lightly flour the top of the dough. Pound it a few times with a rolling pin until it is soft enough to roll, then roll out the dough to about ⅛ inch (3 millimeters).

CUT as many cookies as you can out of the dough with a 2½- to 3-inch (7-centimeter) round cutter and transfer them to the prepared pans. Use a 1-inch (3-centimeter) round cutter to make a small circle in the center of half of the cookies. Repeat with the remaining dough, rerolling the scraps and cut-out centers to get as many cookies as possible. You will need an even number of cookies, half of which will have holes and half of which will not.

BAKE the cookies in the preheated oven until golden brown, about 15 minutes. Allow the cookies to cool completely on the pans on racks.

SPRINKLE the cookies that have the cut-out centers with confectioners' sugar. Turn over the cookies with no cut-out centers so the flat sides are on the top. Spread about ½ teaspoon of jam on each of the inverted cookies. Top with the cut-out cookies, then transfer the remaining jam to a pastry bag and pipe jam into the centers to fill the holes completely.

TORCETTI DI LANZO

TEARDROP COOKIES

Makes about 5 dozen cookies   *Piemonte*

Torcetti (the name means "little twists") from the Piemonte town of Lanzo (hometown of the mother of Katia Delogu, Eataly's executive pastry chef in the U.S.) are made with yeast rather than baking powder. There is no sugar in the dough itself—just a coating on the outside of the cookies that provides a sweet, crisp exterior.

1½ teaspoons (6 grams) active dry yeast or 1 teaspoon (3 grams) instant yeast

½ cup (125 milliliters) warm water

2⅓ cups (250 grams) pastry flour

1 teaspoon (5 grams) salt

7 tablespoons (100 grams) unsalted butter, softened

½ cup (100 grams) sugar

DISSOLVE the active dry yeast in the water. (If using instant yeast, just include it in the dry ingredients.) Place the flour, salt, and butter in the mixing bowl of a stand mixer. Add the yeast and water and beat in the stand mixer fitted with the hook attachment until the dough is well combined and compact, about 5 minutes. Cover the bowl with plastic wrap (or transfer the dough to a clean bowl if you will need the mixing bowl) and refrigerate for at least 8 hours.

REMOVE the dough from the refrigerator, fold it over on itself two to three times, and return it to the bowl. Allow the dough to rest at room temperature until doubled in size, about 2 hours.

LINE baking sheets or jelly-roll pans with parchment paper and set aside.

ROLL out the dough to a thickness of a little less than ½ inch (1 centimeter) and cut into 3½-inch- (9-centimeter-) long strips that are a little less than ½ inch (1 centimeter) wide. Roll each strip out to a cylinder about 6 inches (15 centimeters) long. Dredge the cylinders in the sugar, then shape each sugar-coated cylinder into a teardrop shape by pressing the two ends together and transfer to the prepared pans. Let the cookies rise until they are puffed, 2 to 3 hours.

WHEN you are ready to bake the cookies, preheat the oven to 350°F (180°C), transfer the pans to the oven, and bake until the cookies are well-risen and golden brown, 20 to 25 minutes.

CANESTRELLI
LIGURIAN SHORTBREAD COOKIES

Makes about 2 dozen cookies   *Liguria*

These light shortbread cookies are made with hard-boiled egg yolks. To hard-boil eggs, prepare a bowl of ice water. Place the eggs in a pot with water to cover, bring to a boil, and let the eggs simmer for 8 minutes. Remove from the pot with a slotted spoon or skimmer and dunk immediately in the ice water. Once the eggs are cool, peel them and proceed with the recipe. These cookies may be flavored with lemon or orange zest or with vanilla. Traditionally canestrelli are cut with a special scalloped cookie cutter that makes a hole in the center. You can also use the wide end of a pastry tube to cut the smaller hole in the center, and if all you have is a plain round cookie cutter, they will still taste great.

3 hard-boiled egg yolks

1 stick plus 3 tablespoons (150 grams) unsalted butter, softened

Grated zest of 1 lemon, grated zest of ½ orange, or seeds scraped from ½ vanilla bean

1¼ cups (150 grams) confectioners' sugar, plus more for dusting

2 cups (250 grams) unbleached all-purpose flour

½ teaspoon (2 grams) baking powder

¼ teaspoon (1 gram) salt

PRESS the egg yolks through a fine-mesh strainer into a bowl. Add the softened butter, lemon zest (or orange zest or vanilla), and confectioners' sugar and mix with a wooden spoon until well combined.

IN a separate bowl, sift together the flour, baking powder, and salt. Gradually incorporate the flour mixture into the butter mixture and mix just enough to combine fully. Do not overmix.

SHAPE the dough into a disk, wrap in plastic, and refrigerate for at least 1 hour and up to 3 days.

WHEN you are ready to bake the cookies, preheat the oven to 350°F (180°C). Line baking sheets or jelly-roll pans with parchment paper and set aside.

PLACE a piece of parchment paper on a work surface. Unwrap the dough and place it on the parchment paper. Place another piece of parchment paper on top and roll the dough to ½ inch (1¼ centimeters) thick. Cut out cookies with a 2½-inch (6-centimeter) scalloped cutter and cut out another hole in the center with a 1-inch (2¼-centimeter) round cutter. Transfer to the prepared pans. Bake until the cookies are lightly golden (they should not brown), 10 to 12 minutes. Cool on the pans on racks. Dust with confectioners' sugar just before serving.

ESSE

S-SHAPED GRAPPA COOKIES

Makes about 10 dozen cookies   *Veneto*

Grappa is a strong brandy made from the grape pomace left after winemaking. It is usually enjoyed as a digestivo, but it also gives these crispy cookies a distinctive flavor.

1 stick plus 6 tablespoons (200 grams) unsalted butter, softened

1¼ cups (250 grams) sugar

1 large egg

2 egg yolks

¼ cup (60 milliliters) grappa

1 pinch salt

1½ teaspoons (8 grams) baking powder

Finely grated zest of 1 lemon

4 cups (500 grams) unbleached all-purpose flour

IN a large bowl, cream the butter with the sugar. Lightly beat the whole egg and the yolks together and then beat them into the butter-sugar mixture. Add the grappa, salt, baking powder, lemon zest, and flour. Beat (or knead in the bowl if you are working by hand—the dough will be too thick to stir) until the dough is smooth and well combined. Shape into a ball, wrap in plastic wrap, and refrigerate for 30 minutes.

PREHEAT the oven to 325°F (165°C). Line baking sheets or jelly-roll pans with parchment paper and set aside. Dust a work surface with flour. Pinch off a piece of dough and roll under your palms into a cylinder a little less than ½ inch (1¼ centimeters) in diameter. Cut into 1½-inch (1¼-centimeter) pieces. Roll one piece until it is about 2½ inches (6 to 7 centimeters) long and then transfer to one of the prepared pans, shaping it like an S as you set it down. Bake in the preheated oven until golden brown, about 12 minutes.

OVIS MOLLIS

TENDER COOKIES

Makes about 8 dozen cookies   *Piemonte*

The Latin name of these cookies is a mystery and sounds a little like an incantation, along the lines of "hocus-pocus." No one is sure whether *ovis* is a reference to a sheep or a variation on the Latin word for egg, *ovum*. No matter how they earned the moniker, these are very tender and delicious cookies.

6 hard-boiled egg yolks (see page 14)

1 stick plus 6 tablespoons (200 grams) unsalted butter, softened

¾ cup plus 3 tablespoons (100 grams) confectioners' sugar, plus more for sprinkling

1¾ cups plus 1 tablespoon (200 grams) pastry flour

⅔ cup (100 grams) potato starch

½ teaspoon (5 grams) salt

60 whole, skinned hazelnuts (see page 24) or about 3 tablespoons (60 grams) jam

Confectioners' sugar for sprinkling

FORCE the egg yolks through a fine-mesh sieve and set aside. In a large bowl, beat the butter and sugar together. Beat in the egg yolks. Add the flour, potato starch, and salt and mix until combined, but do not handle the dough any more than necessary. Form the dough into a ball, wrap in plastic, and refrigerate until very cold, at least 3 hours.

PREHEAT the oven to 350°F (180°C). Line baking sheets or jelly-roll pans with parchment paper and set aside. Pinch off a piece of dough and roll under your palms into a cylinder about ½ inch (1¼ centimeters) in diameter. Cut the cylinder into ½-inch (1¼-centimeter) pieces. Pick up one piece and roll between your palms to round it into a ball. Place the balls of dough on the prepared pans. If using hazelnuts, press one whole hazelnut into the center of each cookie, indenting it slightly as you do. If using jam, with your thumb create an indent in each cookie and fill the indent with a dot of the jam. Bake in the preheated oven until firm, 10 to 12 minutes. (They will not color). Cool on the pans on racks. Dust with confectioners' sugar just before serving.

CANTUCCI TOSCANI
TUSCAN ALMOND COOKIES

Makes about 5 dozen cookies   *Toscana*

These almond cookies are baked twice, which makes them extra crisp. They are traditionally served with vin santo, but they are also perfect for dunking in coffee or tea. They will keep for up to a week in a tin with a tight-fitting lid.

1¾ cups (245 grams) raw almonds

5 large eggs

1½ cups (300 grams) sugar

8 tablespoons (1 stick/ 115 grams) unsalted butter, melted and cooled

4¾ cups (500 grams) pastry flour

1 teaspoon (4 grams) baking powder

PREHEAT the oven or a toaster oven to 350°F (180°C).

TOAST the almonds in the preheated oven until fragrant and lightly golden, 8 to 10 minutes. Set aside to cool.

BEAT 4 eggs with the sugar. Pour in the butter and beat until combined. Add the flour and baking powder. Mix until well combined, then stir in the almonds. Refrigerate the dough until firm, about 1 hour.

WHEN you are ready to bake the cookies, preheat the oven to 350°F (180°C). Line baking sheets or jelly-roll pans with parchment paper and set aside.

TRANSFER the dough to a work surface and cut it into two equal portions. Shape each portion of dough into a log the length of the prepared pans. Whisk the remaining egg and brush it lightly onto the tops and sides of the logs, cleaning the brush of excess egg so that you don't drip it down the sides of the logs.

BAKE the logs of dough in the preheated oven for 20 minutes. Allow the logs to cool on the pans set on racks. (You can refrigerate them up to one day at this point if it's more convenient for you to continue at a later time.)

WHEN the logs are cool, use a sharp knife to cut them at an angle into slices about ½ inch (1¼ centimeters) thick. Place the cookies on the pans, cut sides down, and bake at 350°F (180°C), turning once, until golden, about 25 minutes.

AMARETTI

CRISP ALMOND COOKIES

Makes about 4 dozen cookies   *Lombardia*

These classic almond cookies are delicious on their own, but crumbled amaretti are also used as an ingredient in many other dishes. You can roll these in granulated sugar before baking or dust them with confectioners' sugar once they're cool.

2 large egg whites

¾ cup plus 2 tablespoons (170 grams) sugar

2⅓ cups (220 grams) almond flour

Finely grated zest of ½ lemon

PREHEAT the oven to 350°F (180°C). Line baking sheets or jelly-roll pans with parchment paper and set aside.

WHIP the egg whites to a soft peak, then gradually add the sugar while beating to a stiff peak. Fold in the almond flour and lemon zest. The dough should be fairly stiff. Pull off a piece of dough and roll it into a ball about 1 inch (2½ centimeters) in diameter. Place on the prepared pans. Repeat with the remaining dough.

BAKE in the preheated oven until dry and firm, about 40 minutes.

BACI DI DAMA

"LADY'S KISSES" HAZELNUT COOKIES

Makes about 4 dozen sandwich cookies   *Piemonte*

No one is sure why these petite sandwich cookies are called lady's kisses. One theory is that from the side these resemble two lips pressed together tightly, and a true lady doesn't open her mouth while kissing. Another suggests that these are like a lady's kisses because they're delicate and irresistible—just one leaves you wanting more.

18 tablespoons (2 sticks plus 2 tablespoons/250 grams) unsalted butter

1 cup (200 grams) sugar

2 cups (250 grams) unbleached all-purpose flour

2 cups plus 2 tablespoons (250 grams) hazelnut flour

¼ cup (60 grams) giandiua spread

IN a stand mixer fitted with the paddle attachment, beat the butter and sugar. Add the flours about ½ cup (60 grams) at a time, beating to incorporate between additions. Refrigerate the dough until it is very firm, at least 8 hours.

PREHEAT the oven to 275°F (140°C). Line baking sheets or jelly-roll pans with parchment paper and set aside.

ROLL the chilled dough into ropes about ½ inch (1¼ centimeters) in diameter. Cut the ropes into ½-inch (1¼-centimeter) pieces. Roll each piece between the palms of your hands to shape it into a round sphere and transfer to the prepared baking pans with at least 1 inch (2½ centimeters) between them on all sides.

BAKE the cookies in the preheated oven until lightly golden, about 10 minutes. The spheres will flatten on the bottom.

LET the cookies cool completely on the pans on racks.

WHEN the cookies are cool, make a sandwich cookie by spreading about ¼ teaspoon of the gianduia on the flat side of one cookie and gently pressing the flat side of another cookie against it. Repeat with the remaining gianduia and cookies.

OSSA DI MORTO

ALMOND "BONES OF THE DEAD" COOKIES

Makes about 4 dozen cookies

In Italy these are eaten on All Saints' Day, November 1, and All Souls' Day, November 2—which presumably is the source of their name (though some believe the name is a corruption of *ossi da mordere,* or "bones for biting.") Despite any unsettling implications, they are quite tasty!

⅔ cup (100 grams) raw almonds

⅔ cup (100 grams) blanched almonds

1 cup (100 grams) almond flour

¾ cup plus 1 tablespoon (160 grams) sugar

2 egg whites

PREHEAT the oven to 350°F (180°C). Line baking sheets or jelly-roll pans with parchment paper and set aside.

CHOP the raw and blanched almonds into big pieces. (If using a food processor fitted with a metal blade, pulse but do not grind them into a fine powder—there should be a difference between the almond flour and the chopped pieces.)

COMBINE the chopped almonds, almond flour, and sugar and set aside. In a large bowl, whip the egg whites to stiff peaks. Gently fold in the almond and sugar mix, deflating the egg whites as little as possible.

DROP heaping tablespoons of the batter onto the prepared pans. Bake in the preheated oven until the cookies are dry to the touch and lightly browned, about 25 minutes. Cool on the pans on racks.

DOLCI DI OGNISSANTI E IL GIORNO DEI MORTI

Ognissanti, or All Saints' Day, on November 1 is followed by the Giorno dei Morti, or All Souls' Day, on November 2, a day to commemorate family members who have passed away. As in many cultures (think Mexico's Day of the Dead), traditional foods for these holidays reference death in a lighthearted manner. The Ossa di Morto cookies, opposite, are just one of dozens of types of regional cookies prepared for the occasion.

CAVALLI Large sweet buns shaped like their namesake horses (apparently a reference to a Greek goddess who ushered the dead to their final resting places on horseback) are served in Trentino–Alto Adige.

COLVA Also known as the "wheat of the dead," Puglia's colva consists of wheat berries tossed with grapes, pomegranate seeds, and chopped chocolate and sweetened with vin cotto.

DITA DI APOSTOLO In Sicilia locals eat these "apostles' fingers"—made by filling crepes with ricotta and rolling them up—to mark the holiday. Sicilians also make sugar sculptures of the deceased.

FANFULICCHIE Lecce's fanfulicchie are candy spirals of ribbon, typically flavored with mint.

FAVE DEI MORTI In central Italy, the small round cookies known as fave dei morti, or "fava beans of the dead," don't actually contain fava beans or fava flour, but fava beans have been emblems of the souls of the dead since ancient Roman times.

'NZUDDI These wide, flat almond cookies from Sicilia were invented by the Vincentian sisters of Catania, and their name is local dialect for Vincentian.

O' MORTICIELLO Leave it to the residents of Napoli to gild the lily: to honor the dead they make a special chocolate nougat dotted with hazelnuts and then robed in more chocolate.

PAN CO' SANTI In Toscana they feast on a bread dotted with raisins and walnuts and made with lard and honey that resembles Irish soda bread, though it is yeast-risen.

PANE DEI MORTI In Lombardia, amaretti cookie crumbs, cinnamon, nutmeg, and dried fruit are used to make a dense mixture that is pressed, baked, cut into bars, and sprinkled with confectioners' sugar.

PIPARELLE Also known as pipareddi, these cookies hail from the area around Messina on Sicilia. They include almonds, black pepper, and a healthy dose of cloves and are twice-baked like Cantucci Toscani (page 18).

STINCHETTI These "little shin bones" are similar to Ossa di Morto but are made of a firmer dough and each one is modeled to resemble a tibia.

NOCI

We can't resist the pun: In Italy, we're nuts about nuts. In general, unless you are buying nut flour (see page 000), look for whole nuts that are an even color. Nuts contain a lot of oil, so they do have a limited shelf life. Once you get them home, store them in the freezer. Pistachios and pine nuts can go rancid particularly quickly.

MANDORLE

Both bitter and sweet almonds grow in Sicilia. The almonds grown around the town of Noto are highly regarded: they are diminutive, sweet, and meaty. Almonds are a symbol of good fortune, and confetti *(Jordan almonds) are a tradition at weddings in Italy. Almonds are sometimes ground into flour. You can purchase almonds either raw (with the skins) or blanched (peeled), and almonds are also sold slivered and flaked. You can blanch almonds yourself at home, but it is tedious work: place the almonds in boiling water, drain, blot dry, and then squeeze each almond out and discard the skin.*

NOCCIOLE

Italy is a major producer of hazelnuts. While these little round nuts with their peaked tips are grown in several areas of Italy today, they are most closely associated with the Piemonte region. The Tonda Gentile variety is especially sweet. Hazelnut skins can be a bit tenacious. To skin hazelnuts, toast them (see opposite page) and then place them in a clean flat-weave dishtowel and rub them together vigorously. Repeat the process until most of the skins have come off, though a few flecks will always remain attached.

NOCI

Walnuts are also widely used in Italy. The Lara walnuts that grow in Veneto are sweet and meaty, without any of the bitter aftertaste that sometimes affects these popular nuts. The liqueur nocello (sometimes called nocino) is made by macerating green walnuts and has a very rich and layered flavor.

PINOLI

Pine nuts are expensive, but for good reason: they are harvested from pine cones in a labor–intensive process. Pine nuts are used frequently in Italian desserts, but sparingly, perhaps due to the price. They tend to be sprinkled on top of a tart like the Torta della Nonna on page 47 rather than incorporated into fillings in large amounts.

HOW TO TOAST NUTS

Sometimes nuts are toasted to bring out their flavor: Spread the nuts on a baking sheet or jelly-roll pan in a single layer and toast at 350°F (180°C) for about 10 minutes, shaking the pan occasionally. Nuts will grow fragrant as they toast. A toaster oven can be handy, and small amounts can be toasted in a dry pan on the stove, but keep a close eye on them as they quickly go from the perfect brown to burnt.

PISTACCHI

Green pistachios grow in Sicilia; the pistachios from the town of Bronte at the foot of Mount Etna are highly prized. In general, Sicilian pistachios are more elongated and narrow than those you will find elsewhere. They are also more flavorful, thanks to the volcanic soil on the island. Pistachios are also sold in the form of a cream to spread on bread.

RICCIARELLI
CHEWY ALMOND COOKIES

Makes 1 to 2 dozen cookies   *Toscana*

Ricciarelli from Toscana have attractive cracked tops and a pleasantly chewy texture. If you like, you can incorporate tiny cubes of candied orange peel (see page 103) into the dough, and if you really want to go the extra mile, after the ricciarelli have baked and cooled, dip them in melted chocolate.

2 cups (190 grams) almond flour

½ teaspoon (2 grams) baking powder

2 cups (220 grams) confectioners' sugar, plus more for rolling

1 tablespoon (7 grams) unbleached all-purpose flour

2 large egg whites

3 drops almond extract

PREHEAT the oven to 350°F (180°C). Line baking sheets or jelly-roll pans with parchment paper and set aside.

COMBINE the almond flour with the baking powder, 2 cups (220 grams) confectioners' sugar, and flour. Beat the egg whites until they are stiff and fold them into the almond mixture. Add the almond extract and blend the mixture until it forms a soft paste.

DUST a clean, dry work surface with confectioners' sugar. Form one tablespoon of dough into a small ball, then roll it in confectioners' sugar to coat the sides and flatten the cookie slightly with the palm of your hand into an oval. Transfer to one of the prepared baking pans. Repeat with the remaining dough.

BAKE the cookies in the preheated oven until lightly golden, 10 to 12 minutes. Cool completely before serving.

PASTE DI MANDORLA

ALMOND PASTE COOKIES

Makes 2 to 3 dozen cookies

These piped cookies always make a big impression—no one needs to know that they're a breeze to make. If you prefer to use store-bought almond flour rather than grinding the almonds yourself, start with about 2¼ cups (250 grams) of almond flour and be sure to mix it with the sugar very thoroughly before continuing. You will need a very wide tip—at least ½ inch (13 millimeters)—to pipe these, as the dough is quite stiff. It is easier to work with small amounts of dough rather than loading all of it into the bag at once. A cookie press will also work. Or drop spoonfuls of the dough onto cookie sheets and bake; they will be less fancy but equally tasty.

1¾ cups (250 grams) blanched almonds

1¼ cups (250 grams) sugar

3 to 4 drops almond extract

About 2 egg whites

Halved candied cherries, diced candied orange peel (page 103), or whole almonds for decoration

LINE baking sheets or jelly-roll pans with parchment paper and set aside.

IN a food processor fitted with the metal blade, grind the almonds and the sugar to a powder. (Do not overprocess or the nuts will begin to exude oil and the mixture will turn into a paste.) Transfer the almonds and sugar to a bowl and hand knead. Mix in the almond extract and then the egg whites. The mixture should be stiff enough to hold its shape but soft enough to pipe. If it feels too stiff, add a little bit more egg white, about a tablespoon at a time, until it reaches the desired consistency.

FIT a pastry bag with a large open star tip and pipe wreaths, rosettes, or other shapes onto the prepared pans. Decorate with candied cherries, candied orange peel, and almonds.

WRAP the pans with plastic wrap and chill the piped cookies in the refrigerator for 8 hours.

PREHEAT the oven to 325°F (160°C). Bake the cookies until the edges are beginning to darken but the interiors are still pale, about 15 minutes. Cool on the pans on racks.

BISCOTTI SECCHI

Italians have a love for dry cookies with a crisp texture that is softened by dunking. We dip cookies all day long.

MELIGHE

Melighe cookies hail from Piemonte. These ridged cornmeal butter cookies have great snap. Italy's first prime minister, Torino native Camillo Benso, is said to have concluded every meal he ate with a few melighe dipped in local Barolo.

BISCOTTI PER COLAZIONE

This is a category of cookies with a special place in the heart of every Italian: breakfast cookies. Biscotti per colazione tend to be crisp, plain, and not too sweet—perfect for dipping in a cappuccino or a bowl of steamed milk.

CANTUCCI

*Toscana's famed almond cantucci
(page 18) are baked twice, giving them
a particularly resistant texture.*

AMARETTI

*Amaretti are always made with almonds,
but they may have a crisp or a slightly chewy
texture. The crisp amaretti from Saronno in
Lombardia—sold in a signature bright-red
tin—are world-famous. Two or three of these
make a satisfying afternoon snack. See the recipe
on page 20 if you'd like to make your own.*

HOW TO DIP CANTUCCI IN VIN SANTO

Tuscany's traditional twice-baked cookies like the cantucci on page 18 are dipped in vin santo, sweet dessert wine, to soften them.

1. Pour vin santo into a glass with a wide mouth (not a champagne glass) to a depth of two to three fingers.

2. Pick up a cookie. Holding one end of the cookie, immerse an inch or two of the other end in the glass. Hold for a count of five.

3. Eat softened portion of cookie. Repeat.

TORTE

Any get–together is improved
with a slice of cake or tart.

ATTREZZI E UTENSILI

Italian baking doesn't require a lot of fancy equipment, but there are certain basic tools that are needed to craft even humble cakes and tarts.

SIEVE A small conical sieve with fine mesh makes it a breeze to sift confectioners' sugar over a finished cake or tart.

BRUSH You'll need a pastry brush for delicate touches such as applying an egg wash to a dough for an appealingly shiny finish.

PASTRY WHEEL A pastry wheel may be fluted or straight and is useful for cutting doughs.

TUBES Metal cylinders are used as forms for shaping Cannoli (page 93) and Cannoncini (page 99). A sturdy set will last indefinitely. Cone-shaped forms are also available.

WHISKS Hand-held whisks (also known as whips) come in dozens of styles. As an all-purpose tool, we favor the type known as a French whisk, which is longer and narrower than the round balloon whisk. It is great for getting right up against the side of a bowl. The wires of a whisk should be slightly flexible.

BEATERS Stand and hand-held mixers usually come with several attachments. A stand mixer has a balloon whisk attachment; a hand-held mixer is typically equipped with a pair of sturdy stainless-steel beaters.

CAKE PAN If you are an enthusiastic baker, you will accumulate cake pans of all shapes and sizes, but to our mind the most useful and basic is a 9-inch (23-centimeter) round pan with 2-inch (5-centimeter) sides.

PASTRY BAG AND PIPING TUBES Pastry bags and piping tubes are useful for piping cookies such as Granellati (page 8) as well as creating whipped cream and pastry cream rosettes and other simple decorations. Disposable plastic bags are convenient, and if you can have just two tubes, purchase one star-shaped tube and one plain tube. The larger end of a pastry tube can also be used to cut out the centers of ring-shaped cookies such as Occhi di Bue (page 10).

AMOR POLENTA

POLENTA POUND CAKE

Makes one 9 x 5 x 3-inch (21 x 11 x 7-centimeter) loaf cake,
about 12 slices   *Lombardia*

Amor polenta—literally "polenta love," which should give you some idea of the passion this cake inspires—is traditionally made in a ridged pan so that it looks a bit like a caterpillar. It will taste just as good when baked in a traditional loaf pan. The polenta in this cake is not the coarsely ground type used to make the dish also known as polenta, but the most finely ground cornmeal you can find, sometimes labeled as "corn flour" in the United States. (Elsewhere in the English-speaking world, corn flour is what we would call cornstarch.)

Cooking spray for pan

7 tablespoons (100 grams) unsalted butter, softened

½ cup plus 2 tablespoons (120 grams) sugar

2 large eggs

¾ cup (100 grams) finely ground cornmeal

¾ cup (80 grams) pastry flour

¾ cup (70 grams) almond flour

2½ teaspoons (10 grams) baking powder

1 tablespoon (20 grams) Grand Marnier, optional

PREHEAT the oven to 350°F (180°C). Spray a 9 × 5 × 3-inch (21 × 11 × 7-centimeter) loaf pan with vegetable oil and set aside.

IN a large bowl beat the butter with the sugar until soft and fluffy. Add the eggs one at a time, beating to incorporate between additions. Beat in the cornmeal, pastry flour, almond flour, and baking powder. Stir in the Grand Marnier, if using.

TRANSFER the batter to the prepared pan and bake until the top is golden and a tester emerges clean, about 35 minutes. Cool in the pan on the rack for about 10 minutes, then unmold and cool completely on the rack.

DOLCI DI POLENTA

THE WORD POLENTA HAS TWO MEANINGS: it indicates the dish of cooked cornmeal mush served in northern Italy, and it also indicates the cornmeal used to make that dish. While polenta today has reached a fairly elevated status, it actually was originally—like so many Italian specialties—the food of the poor. Families that could not afford relatively pricey wheat flour ate polenta instead. They cooked the cornmeal into porridge that they topped with savory stews (or maybe just a drizzle of oil), but they also used it in place of flour in various desserts. Cornmeal lends all kinds of sweets a slightly sandy texture that we adore. It is also highly absorbent—you will notice that desserts made with polenta usually require a larger amount of liquid than flour-based cakes.

PINZA FROM THE VENETO is traditionally eaten on the Epiphany, January 6. It is a cake, sometimes as much as three feet long, made with polenta and figs. It is baked in the oven, then cooled completely before serving.

TO MAKE FRITTELLE DI POLENTA, or polenta fritters, stir finely grated lemon and orange zest, a pinch of baking powder, sugar, eggs, and milk into cooked polenta until it forms a slurry. Let it rest for about 30 minutes, then form small balls of the mixture with two spoons and fry them in oil until golden. Sprinkle with confectioners' sugar or granulated sugar and serve hot.

VENETO'S FAMED ZALETTI COOKIES (the name is dialect for "little yellow ones") are crisp cornmeal cookies with raisins.

TORTA ALL'OLIO D'OLIVA
OLIVE OIL CAKE

Makes one 9-inch ring cake, about 12 servings

Olive oil creates a tender, moist crumb in a cake. If you like you can sift some confectioners' sugar over the cake just before serving.

3 large eggs

¾ cup plus 2 tablespoons (180 grams) sugar

3 tablespoons (50 milliliters) whole milk

¼ cup plus 3 tablespoons (100 milliliters) extra-virgin olive oil

2⅓ cups (250 grams) pastry flour

⅓ cup (50 grams) potato starch

2½ teaspoons (10 grams) baking powder

Finely grated zest of 1 lemon

PREHEAT the oven to 325°F (160°C). Oil or butter a 9-inch ring pan and set aside.

WHISK the eggs with the sugar until they are smooth and a pale yellow. Gradually add the milk while whisking constantly, then the oil, still whisking constantly. Sift in the flour, starch, and baking powder, then add the lemon zest and stir to combine.

POUR the batter into the prepared pan and bake until it is golden and a cake tester in the center of the ring emerges clean, about 35 minutes. Cool in the pan on the rack for about 10 minutes, then unmold and cool completely.

TORTA TENERINA

TENDER CHOCOLATE CAKE

Makes one 9-inch (23-centimeter) cake, about 12 servings   *Emilia-Romagna*

Torta tenerina, as its name implies, is an extremely tender cake. As it bakes, a crackly crust forms on top, but the interior remains soft and creamy. This cake hails from Ferrara, where it is also known as torta taclenta, which means "sticky cake" in the local dialect. Use a spatula to fold the ingredients together gently, maintaining as much volume as possible. Keep in mind that you want the center to be very soft, so the usual technique for testing doneness by inserting a toothpick or skewer won't work. And never use your oven's convection setting for this cake—you want the air to circulate as little as possible while it is baking.

9 large eggs, separated

2⅓ cups (300 grams) confectioners' sugar, plus more for dusting

¼ cup (30 grams) unbleached all-purpose flour, plus more for flouring pan

3 tablespoons (30 grams) potato starch

10½ ounces (300 grams) bittersweet chocolate

2 sticks plus 2 tablespoons (260 grams) unsalted butter, plus more for the pan

PREHEAT the oven to 350°F (180°C). Butter and flour (or use cocoa powder) a 9-inch (23-centimeter) cake pan, preferably a springform, and set aside.

BEAT the egg yolks with the confectioners' sugar, ¼ cup (30 grams) flour, and potato starch until combined. Place the chocolate and 2 sticks plus 2 tablespoons (260 grams) butter in the top of a double boiler and melt, then whisk to combine. Allow to cool. Beat the egg whites to a stiff peak. Fold the egg whites into the chocolate mixture in three additions, then gently fold in the flour mixture until well combined.

TRANSFER the batter to the prepared pan and bake in the preheated oven until a crust has formed on top and the middle has just set, 45 to 50 minutes. Allow to cool in the pan. Dust with confectioners' sugar just before serving.

PAN DI SPAGNA

SPONGE CAKE

Makes one 18 x 13-inch (46 x 33-centimeter) and ¾-inch- (2-centimeter-) high rectangular layer or two 9-inch (23-centimeter) round and 1½-inch- (3¾-centimeter-) high round layers

The soft Italian sponge cake known as Pan di Spagna, or "bread of Spain," is probably the most frequently made cake in Italy. It isn't often eaten on its own, but it is a component in many other recipes, such as Trancetti Diplomatici (page 90), zuccotto, cassata, and zuppa inglese. We like to make Pan di Spagna with rice flour. It results in a lighter, fluffier layer that is also gluten-free. See opposite for suggestions about what to do with the cake after you've baked it. If you want to bake a single tall, round layer, you will need a baking pan with 3-inch (8 centimeter) sides, or create a collar around the pan with parchment as you would for a soufflé, as—much like a soufflé—the cake puffs up as it bakes.

6 large eggs, separated

3 egg whites

1½ cups (300 grams) sugar

1¾ cups (240 grams) rice flour

2 tablespoons (20 grams) cornstarch

PREHEAT the oven to 350°F (180°C). Line a baking sheet or jelly-roll pan or 2 round cake pans with parchment paper, or butter and flour two springform pans and set aside.

WHIP the 9 egg whites with the sugar until billowy and glossy and greatly increased in volume, about 10 minutes. Separately, whisk the 6 egg yolks until light yellow. Using a spatula, fold the egg yolks into the egg whites. Sift the rice flour and cornstarch over the egg mixture in three

additions, folding between additions. Gently spread the mixture in the prepared pan or pans, deflating it as little as possible. Smooth the top. Bake in the preheated oven until the cake springs back when pressed with a fingertip, about 20 minutes for a layer on a baking sheet or jelly-roll pan and 30 minutes for round layers. Cool completely in the pan on a rack.

WHEN the cake is cool, for a baking sheet or jelly-roll pan, set another baking sheet or jelly-roll pan on top (bottom down) and flip the two pans together. Remove the pan on top and gently peel the parchment paper off the baked layer. Slide the layer off the back of the pan onto a work surface. For a round pan, do the same, inverting the cake onto a plate or rack, peeling off the paper, then turning it right side up. For a springform pan, simply unbuckle the outer ring and gently slide the cake onto the work surface.

VARIATION: **PAN DI SPAGNA AL CACAO** Sift ⅓ cup (35 grams) cocoa powder in along with the flour.

Once you've got your Pan di Spagna, the possibilities are limitless. Here are just a few ideas for using this versatile cake:

BRUSH THE LAYER WITH A SUGAR SYRUP OR LIQUEUR, cut the layer into pieces, and use some of the pieces to line a bowl lined with plastic wrap. Fill the cake-lined bowl with flavored Crema Pasticcera (page 88), then cover the top with more pieces of cake, cutting to fit. Refrigerate until firm, then flip and unmold. Decorate with whipped cream.

MAKE AN ESPRESSO SYRUP by boiling espresso and sugar until reduced. Brush the cake with the syrup, then top with whipped cream. (This is delicious with the cocoa powder variation, or sprinkle some cocoa powder on top of the whipped cream.)

SPREAD JAM BETWEEN TWO LAYERS. Sprinkle with confectioners' sugar just before serving.

CUT THE LAYER INTO RECTANGLES THAT WILL FIT IN A LOAF PAN. (If you know you want to use your pan di Spagna this way, you can even bake it in a buttered and floured loaf pan and you'll have the perfect sized and shaped cake.) Puree raspberries and strain out the seeds. Brush the layers with simple syrup and make alternating layers of cake and raspberry puree in a plastic-lined loaf pan. Refrigerate until firm, then invert, unmold and slice to reveal the pretty stripes.

MINI SBRISOLONE

CRUMBLY ALMOND TARTLETS

Makes 8 individual tarts   *Lombardia*

A sbrisolona is a very crumbly tart, more like a giant cookie than what we usually think of as a cake. A large sbrisolona does not cut into neat slices but instead breaks into rough shards, so at Eataly's pastry counter we serve small individual sbrisolone. If you prefer to make one large tart, simply press the mixture into a buttered 9-inch (23-centimeter) springform pan and bake for about 25 minutes, then cool completely before unbuckling the ring and serving.

1¾ cups plus 2 table-spoons (200 grams) pastry flour

1½ cups (200 grams) finely ground cornmeal

¾ cup plus 2 tablespoons (180 grams) sugar

1 cup (100 grams) almond flour

2 teaspoons (10 grams) baking powder

½ teaspoon (5 grams) salt

1 stick plus 6 tablespoons (200 grams) unsalted butter, cold, plus more for the pan

2 large eggs

Finely grated zest of 1 lemon

1 cup (100 grams) toasted almonds (see page 000)

PREHEAT the oven to 350°F (180°C). Line a baking sheet or jelly-roll pan with parchment paper and set aside.

IN a large bowl whisk together the pastry flour, cornmeal, sugar, almond flour, baking powder, and salt. Cut the cold butter into cubes and add it to the bowl, then blend by hand or with a pastry cutter until the mixture resembles sand and pebbles.

WHISK together the eggs and lemon zest, then use your hands to incorporate this egg mixture into the dough. It will look very dry and crumbly but will begin to clump together.

PLACE a 3-inch (8-centimeter) ring mold on the prepared pan. Place one-eighth of the mixture in the ring mold and press down to form a disk. Scatter one-eighth of the toasted almonds on top and press them gently into the dough. Slip off the ring mold and repeat with the remaining dough and toasted almonds. Bake in the preheated oven until the tartlets are golden brown and dry, about 20 minutes. Cool completely on the pan and remove with a wide spatula to serve—they are very delicate.

CROSTATA DI NOCI E MIELE

HONEY NUT TART

Makes one 9-inch (23-centimeter) tart, 8 to 10 servings

Nocello is walnut liqueur. It adds a rich, nuanced flavor to this nutty filling. Both the dough and the filling can be made a day in advance.

¼ cup plus 2 tablespoons (135 grams) acacia honey

¼ cup plus 2 tablespoons (85 grams) sugar

¾ cup plus 2 tablespoons (200 grams) heavy cream, warm

1¾ cups (200 grams) chopped walnuts

1 tablespoon (20 milliliters) nocello

1 batch (500 grams) Pasta Frolla (page 67)

FOR the filling, combine the honey, sugar, and 3 tablespoons (50 millimeters) water in a large pot. (The honey will bubble up when the cream is added.) Cook, whisking frequently, over medium-low heat, until golden. Slowly add the cream in a thin stream, whisking constantly. When all the cream has been incorporated, stir in the nuts. Transfer the filling to a bowl and allow it to cool to room temperature, then stir in the liqueur and refrigerate for at least 4 hours and up to 3 days.

WHEN you are ready to bake the tart, preheat the oven to 350°F (180°C). Reserve about one-third of the dough. On a lightly floured surface, roll out the remaining dough ¼ to ⅛ inch (4 millimeters) thick. Line a 9-inch (23-centimeter) cake pan or pie pan with the dough, fitting it against the sides and about 1 inch (2½ centimeters) up the sides. Spread the filling in an even layer on the dough. Roll out the remaining dough and use it to create a lattice. (See pages 76–77.) Place the cake pan on a baking sheet or jelly-roll pan (the filling can bubble up and overflow during baking) and bake in the preheated oven until the crust is golden, about 25 minutes. Cool on a rack before serving.

TORTA DELLA NONNA

PINE NUT TART

Makes one 9-inch (23-centimeter) tart, 8 to 10 servings

This tart is known all over Italy as "grandmother's tart." It's not clear whose grandmother first made it, but she had good taste. This can be baked in any type of pan you like—a cake pan, a springform, a pie tin, or even a tart pan with a removable bottom, though you may not be able to fit all of the crema pasticerra in a tart pan.

Butter for the pan

½ batch (250 grams) Pasta Frolla (page 67)

2 cups (500 grams) Crema Pasticcera (page 88)

½ cup (75 grams) pine nuts

Confectioners' sugar for dusting

PREHEAT the oven to 350°F (180°C). Butter a 9-inch (23-centimter) pan and set aside.

ON a lightly floured surface, roll out the dough to about ¼ inch (½ centimeter) thick and use it to line the prepared pan on the bottom and about 1 inch (2½ centimeters) up the sides, pressing it into the corners. Spread the pastry cream in the dough, then scatter the pine nuts in a single layer on top of the pastry cream. Bake in the preheated oven until the crust is golden brown, the nuts are toasted, and the filling is firm, about 35 minutes. Serve slightly warm and sprinkle with confectioners' sugar just before serving.

MERINGATA ALLE FRAGOLE

STRAWBERRY MERINGUE TORTE

Makes one 8-inch (20-centimeter) cake, about 8 servings

Meringue must bake low and slow. The idea is for the base to be stiff and dry without browning. Once you learn the easy technique for making meringue disks, you can do dozens of different things with them. They can be layered with pastry cream (with or without chopped fruit folded into it) rather than, or in addition to, whipped cream. If you are uncertain about forming an even circle, use a pencil to trace a cake pan or other round item on the back of the parchment paper to use as a guide. And if you want to make a meringue dessert in advance and don't want it to get soggy as it sits, brush the skimpiest layer of melted white chocolate on the meringue and it will serve as a barrier.

⅔ cup (125 grams) granulated sugar

2½ cups (250 grams) confectioners' sugar

4 egg whites

1 pound (400 grams) strawberries, hulled

1 cup (240 grams) whipping cream

PREHEAT the oven to 210°F (100°C). Line a baking sheet or jelly-roll pan with parchment paper and set aside.

WHILE the oven is preheating, combine the granulated sugar and 1¼ cups (125 grams) of the confectioners' sugar in a bowl. Add half the sugar mixture to the egg whites and beat them to very firm peaks with an electric mixer. When the mixture becomes firm and shiny, slowly incorporate the remaining half of the sugar mixture.

FILL a pastry bag fitted with a smooth tip with the meringue mixture and pipe two disks 8 inches (20 centimeters) in diameter on the prepared pan. Pipe the remaining meringue off to the side of the pan. (The shape doesn't matter, as you're going to crumble this meringue.) Place the meringues in the oven and bake, leaving the door partially open, until dry to the touch, about 3 hours. Cool on the pan on a rack.

FOR the filling, place half the strawberries in a food processor fitted with the metal blade and blend into a smooth puree. Beat the whipping cream with the remaining 1¼ cups (125 grams) confectioners' sugar until soft and fluffy. Fold in the berry puree.

PLACE one of the meringue disks on a serving dish and spread about a third of the whipped cream mixture

over it. Place halved strawberries on top of the cream.
Crumble the remaining meringue and press it against
the sides. Top with the second meringue disk. Using a
pastry bag, pipe the remaining whipped cream mixture
on the meringue and top with the remaining strawberries. Chill the assembled dessert in the refrigerator until
ready to serve. Slice just before serving.

MILLEFOGLIE

THOUSAND-LAYER CAKE

Makes one 9- or 10-inch cake, 6 to 8 servings

At Eataly, we make this attractive millefoglie cake (a favorite birthday cake in Italy) with round puff-pastry layers interspersed with delicious pastry cream. Store this cake in the refrigerator, but it's best made shortly before serving as the pastry begins to grow soggy if it sits for too long.

1 pound (485 grams) Pasta Sfoglia (page 52), divided into 3 equal pieces, or 3 sheets store-bought puff pastry

2 cups (500 grams) Crema Pasticcera (page 88)

1 cup (240 grams) heavy cream

2 tablespoons (25 grams) granulated sugar

Confectioners' sugar for sprinkling

1 strawberry, halved

PREHEAT the oven to 350°F (180°C). Roll out the puff pastry less than ⅒ inch (2 millimeters) thick. Place the sheets and any scraps on parchment paper–lined baking sheets or jelly-roll pans and prick all over with a fork. Bake in the preheated oven until golden and puffed (but if sheets are puffing too much prick with a fork again), 10 to 15 minutes. Remove and let the pastry cool on the pans on racks. With a serrated knife, trim the cooked pastry into disks 9 to 10 inches (23 to 25 centimeters) in diameter. (It can be useful to use a cake pan or cardboard as a guide.) Reserve scraps. Don't worry if your disks are slightly uneven—the whipped cream will cover all flaws!

PLACE one pastry disk on a serving plate. Spread half the crema pasticcera on top and cover with another disk. Spread with the remaining crema pasticcera on top of the second disk and cover with the third disk. Whip the cream with the granulated sugar. Frost the top and sides of the cake with the whipped cream. Crush the cooked puff-pastry scraps into crumbs and gently press them against the top and sides of the cake. Sprinkle with confectioners' sugar, top with the strawberry, and serve.

PASTA SFOGLIA

PUFF PASTRY

Makes about 1 pound (485 grams) dough

The idea of making your own puff pastry might sound intimidating, but there is nothing complicated about it. It is, however, time consuming to make puff pastry using the classic method, because you need to keep refrigerating the dough in between folds so that the butter doesn't get too soft. Plan ahead. The instructions below are for completing two turns at a time, but if at any time the butter seems to be smearing (this tends to happen in warm weather, or even on a day when your oven has been on for a long time and is heating up the kitchen), rewrap the dough and refrigerate it until firm, about 30 minutes. Finished dough can be refrigerated for a few days or frozen for up to two weeks. You can also buy frozen sheets of puff pastry that are quite good. Be sure to select a puff pastry that uses only butter. Packaged puff pastry is sold in sheets, already rolled out and ready to be trimmed and baked. Remember always to roll puff pastry with the layers horizontal.

1 stick plus 6 tablespoons (200 grams) unsalted butter, cold

1½ cups (180 grams) bread flour

1 teaspoon (5 grams) salt

½ cup (120 milliliters) cold water

FIRST make a butter block. Arrange the butter on the work surface on a piece of parchment paper to form a rectangle. (In other words, you may have to cut the longer stick into pieces and line the sticks up in two rows that are basically even.) Fold the parchment paper over the top of the butter. With a rolling pin (or a meat tenderizer) pound the butter to form a square, rotating it to keep the shape even. The goal is to have a single block of butter that is relatively consistent (the same height throughout) and flexible enough that it does not break when you bend it. The finished square should have sides about 4 to 5 inches (10 to 13 centimeters) long. Wrap the butter (you can use the parchment) and refrigerate while you make the dough and until it is chilled but still flexible, about 20 minutes.

FOR the dough, combine the flour, salt, and cold water in a large bowl. Knead into a smooth dough, then refrigerate the dough as well if the butter is not yet chilled. When you are ready to proceed, roll the dough into a rough square (about 9 inches or 23 centimeters per side) on a lightly floured work surface. Place the cold butter block in the center of the dough and fold the sides in over the butter, then fold the bottom of the dough up and the top down so that no butter is visible. Flip the package over, seam side down. (Lightly flour the work surface and the dough again if necessary.) Roll the dough to a rectangle about 12 × 8-inches (30 × 20-centimeters). Fold the bottom up and the top down, like folding a letter. Turn the dough a quarter turn so that it is now perpendicular to its original position (with the seam running down the middle toward you). Dust the dough and surface again if necessary and roll out the dough to a rectangle about ½ inch (1½ centimeters) thick. Fold the bottom up and top down, wrap, and refrigerate for 30 minutes to 1 hour. Repeat this process a total of three times (for a total of six turns), refrigerating between every two folds or more often if necessary. By the time you are completing the final turns, the dough will be layered and smooth. Refrigerate the dough overnight.

PASTA SFOGLIA VELOCE

YOU CAN MAKE A QUICKER VERSION OF PUFF PASTRY, also known as "rough puff," by cutting the butter into small pieces; it is helpful to have everything, even the flour, very cold when using this method. (Some people freeze the butter and then grate it on the large holes of a four-sided grater.) Combine the flour and salt and work in about one-third of the cold butter the way you would for a pie crust, but not breaking down the butter too far—you should still see visible chunks. Then stir in the water (which must be very cold) and form a rough dough. Refrigerate until firm, then roll out into a rectangle about 12 × 8-inches (30× 20-centimeters), scatter about half the remaining butter on the surface of the center of the rectangle, and fold the bottom up and the top down. Make a quarter turn so that the seam is running down the middle toward you and roll to ½ inch (1½ centimeters) thick and fold again. Refrigerate, then place seam perpendicular to you, roll into a rectangle ½ inch (1½ centimeters) thick, scatter on the remaining butter, and fold. Turn, roll, and fold two additional times without adding any more butter, then wrap and refrigerate for at least 3 hours before rolling and baking. This version is not quite as flaky as the classic version, but it is still delicious.

PASTA SFOGLIA

Once you've made your puff pastry, the hard part is over and the fun begins. Flaky puff pastry dough can be used to make all kinds of treats. It can be cut into any shape you desire or left whole and used to line a tart or pie pan or a jelly-roll pan. Either bake the pastry in advance and fill it, or use it as a wrapper or crust. Just a few sweet suggestions:

CORNETTI Cut a puff pastry layer into triangles. Dab a little jam in the middle of each triangle. Roll up into a cylinder, starting with the wide end, and shape into a crescent. Sprinkle with sugar and bake at 350°F (180°C) until golden, about 15 minutes.

FAGOTTINI DI MELE Cook diced apples and sugar until they have given up their liquid. Cut puff pastry into squares. Place a spoonful of the apple mixture (remove from the pot with a slotted spoon to leave liquid behind) to one side of each square. Brush some of the apple liquid around the perimeter of the square, then fold the pastry over the filling to form a rectangle. Cut a few slits in the top of each pastry, brush with more cooking liquid, and bake at 425°F (220°C) until golden, 10 to 15 minutes.

SFOGLIATINE DI VILLAFRANCA Villafranca, just outside of Verona, is known for these simple puff pastry rings. With a round cutter cut disks of puff pastry. With a smaller round cutter cut a disk from the center of each to make a ring. Brush the rings with egg yolk, sprinkle with a generous amount of sugar, and bake at 400°F (200°C) until the sugar has caramelized, about 20 minutes.

SPORCAMUSS These desserts are called "face dirtiers" for good reason, but they're worth the effort it takes to eat them! Cut a layer of puff pastry into squares, prick with a fork, and bake at 350°F (180°C) until golden and crisp. Cool, then form sandwiches filled with diplomat cream (page 89). Sprinkle generously with confectioners' sugar just before serving.

VENTAGLIETTI Also known as palmiers or elephant ears, these "little fans" are best served warm and crisp. Sprinkle sugar on the work surface and place a layer of puff pastry on top of it. Sprinkle the top with sugar and very gently roll over it with a rolling pin to help the sugar adhere. (You don't want to thin the dough.) Roll up the two ends to meet in the middle like a scroll and chill until firm. Cut into ½-inch (1½-centimeter) slices, dip both cut sides in sugar, and place pastries on their cut sides on baking sheets or jelly-roll pans. Bake at 400°F (200°C) until the sugar has caramelized, about 20 minutes.

TORTA DI NOCCIOLE

HAZELNUT CAKE

Makes one 9-inch cake, about 12 servings   *Piemonte*

Italians are crazy for nut cakes of all kinds—almond, walnut, and especially hazelnut. These cakes keep beautifully and are perfect for breakfast, an afternoon snack, or dessert. A bit of cocoa powder adds another dimension to this cake. See page 24 for instructions on toasting and skinning hazelnuts, but don't worry about removing every last shred of skin—this is a rustic cake that doesn't require that level of perfection.

1²/₃ cups (250 grams) hazelnuts, toasted and skinned (see page 24)

1 stick plus 3 tablespoons (150 grams) unsalted butter, softened, plus more for the pan

¾ cup (150 grams) sugar

4 large eggs

½ cup (50 grams) pastry flour

2½ teaspoons (10 grams) baking powder

1 tablespoon plus 1 teaspoon (10 grams) cocoa powder

PREHEAT the oven to 350°F (180°C). Grind 1 cup (150 grams) of the hazelnuts into flour. (You can also replace this amount of the whole hazelnuts with 1 cup hazelnut flour.) Chop the remaining ⅔ cup (100 grams) finely, but don't grind them to a powder.

BUTTER a 9-inch round cake pan, line the bottom with a parchment paper circle, and butter the parchment. Scatter the finely chopped ⅔ cup (100 grams) hazelnuts in the bottom of the pan and turn the pan so they adhere to the sides. Shake out the excess and reserve.

BEAT the butter and sugar until light and fluffy. Add the eggs one at a time, beating to incorporate between additions, then add the pastry flour, baking powder, cocoa powder, and the reserved finely ground hazelnuts. Transfer to the prepared pan. Scatter the reserved whole hazelnuts on top. Bake until the cake is golden and a tester emerges clean, about 30 minutes. Cool in the pan on a rack for about 10 minutes, then invert, unmold, peel off the parchment paper, and cool completely.

LA FARINA

Farina, or flour, is simply a ground powder, most often of wheat but sometimes other items, such as nuts, as well. Polenta (see page 38) is another type of flour used in Italian baking.

FARINA oo

This is Italy's all-purpose flour. In Italy we grade flours by the extraction rate, meaning how much of the bran and germ have been removed, and OO is the most highly refined. It is also finely ground, and if you pinch a little, it feels silky, never sandy or gritty.

FARINA DI RISO

Rice flour is gluten-free and results in a very light mouth feel when used in baked goods. It can lend a crumbly, slightly sandy texture that is desirable in items such as shortbread. It is also sometimes used as a coating on fried foods, as it fries up very crisp.

FARINA DI CASTAGNE

Chestnut flour is made by grinding dry-roasted chestnuts to a powder. You can make your own nut flours very easily in a food processor fitted with a metal blade. Just be sure not to grind nuts into a paste, as they begin to release their oils and clump together. At Eataly we also carry almond flour and hazelnut flour.

FARINA INTEGRALE

Whole wheat flour has not had the bran, endosperm, and germ of the wheat sifted out. (It is at the opposite end of the extraction spectrum from farina 00.) This gives it a wheatier taste and a darker color. Whole wheat flour often results in a crumbly texture, but its distinctive flavor is delicious in more rustic desserts.

FARINA DI GRAN SARACENO

Buckwheat is not actually a grain but a grass, and buckwheat flour has no gluten. It has a dense texture and a distinctive flavor—some people liken it to the taste of beer.

FARINA DI GRANO TENERO

Pastry flour is made from soft (low-protein) wheat. Because it is low in gluten, it creates lofty cakes with a tender crumb.

FARINA DI PANE

Bread flour is made by milling high-protein wheat. It is considered "strong" because of its protein content, which means it contains a large amount of gluten and easily forms an elastic dough. In Italy, high-protein flour is often labeled farina Manitoba or farina d'America, as it is typically made using a strain of wheat that was first grown in Canada.

DOLCI ALLA FRUTTA

*Fruit is the perfect everyday sweet in its
natural state, but it is an unbeatable
component in more elaborate desserts.*

BRUSTENGO UMBRO

SWEET POLENTA FROM UMBRIA

Makes 1 dozen cakes   *Umbria*

These individual polenta cakes made with fresh and dried fruit and nuts are as comforting as they come. They are delicious with a scoop of gelato or drizzled with honey. You can also spread the mixture on a buttered half-sheet pan or in a buttered round cake pan and bake it as one large cake to cut into squares or wedges.

¾ cup (115 grams) raisins

Butter for the pan

1¾ cups (300 grams) polenta

2 cups boiling water

1 cup (240 milliliters) whole milk

2 tablespoons (30 grams) unsalted butter, melted

¾ cup (150 grams) sugar

¼ teaspoon (2 grams) salt

1 large apple, peeled, cored, and diced

¾ cup (75 grams) walnuts, chopped

¼ cup (35 grams) pine nuts

Grated zest of 1 lemon

PREHEAT the oven to 350°F (180°C). Soak the raisins in cold water for 10 minutes. Drain and set aside. Butter a muffin tin and set aside.

PLACE the polenta in a large pot over low heat. Add the boiling water in a thin stream, stirring constantly with a wooden spoon. Add the milk in a thin stream, stirring constantly. Continue to stir while adding the butter, sugar, salt, diced apple, drained raisins, walnuts, pine nuts, and lemon zest. Stir constantly over low heat for 10 minutes. The mixture will be quite dense.

DIVIDE the mixture among the indentations of the prepared pan. (You can fill the muffin cups all the way to the top, as these don't rise.) Smooth the tops with an offset spatula or the palm of your hand. Set aside to rest at room temperature for 10 minutes.

BAKE in the preheated oven until firm and golden, 40 to 50 minutes. Remove from the oven and cool in the pan for 10 minutes, then run a butter knife around the outside of each cake and unmold. Serve warm or at room temperature.

TORTA DI MELE E BURRO NOCCIOLA

APPLE BROWN-BUTTER CAKE

Makes one 9- or 10-inch (23- or 25-centimeter) cake, 8 to 10 servings

Browning butter gives this cake a rich, nutty flavor with hints of caramel. It's easy to do, and the brown butter really enhances a simple cake like this one. This is equally delicious when made with pears.

2 sticks (220 grams) unsalted butter, plus more for the pan

2 apples

¼ cup (50 grams) packed brown sugar

3 egg whites

¾ cup plus 1 tablespoon (165 grams) granulated sugar

½ teaspoon (5 grams) salt

1 cup (100 grams) almond flour

¾ cup (80 grams) pastry flour

TO brown the butter, place the 2 sticks of butter in a small light-colored pot (if the pot is dark you will not be able to judge the color of the butter) and place over low heat. Melt the butter, stirring frequently. First the butter will foam, and then it will begin to darken. Keep a close eye on the butter—it can go from nicely brown to burnt very quickly. It should be a deep golden caramel color. If the butter does develop dark flecks, strain them out with a sieve. Remove the butter from the heat and allow to cool completely.

POACH THE APPLES: Peel the apples, halve them, and place the apple halves in a pot with the brown sugar. Add water just to cover. Bring to a boil, then simmer until the apples are soft enough to pierce with a paring knife but still hold their shape, about 3 minutes. Cool the apples completely in the syrup, then core and thinly slice. Return the slices to any remaining syrup until you are ready to use them.

WHEN you are ready to bake the cake, preheat the oven to 350°F (180°C). Butter a 9- or 10-inch (23- or 25-centimeter) cake or springform pan and set aside. Beat the egg whites in a stand mixer with the whisk attachment. When the egg whites begin to firm, gradually add the sugar and salt and beat until they form stiff peaks. Fold in the flours and the cooled browned butter. Remove the apple slices from the syrup. Set aside a few slices for decoration and fold the rest, along with any syrup that clings to them, into the egg white mixture.

TRANSFER the batter to the prepared pan, arrange the reserved apple slices decoratively on top, and bake until the top is golden and a tester emerges clean—start testing after 35 minutes, though the cake may take as long as 45 minutes depending on the pan size and amount of syrup. Cool in the pan on a rack.

CROSTATA DI PERE CON CREMA COTTA

PEAR AND CUSTARD TART

Makes one 9-inch (23-centimeter) tart, 8 to 10 servings

Pears and custard are a match made in heaven. Bosc and Anjou pears are a good choice for this tart as they don't dissolve when cooked. If you like, use a spoon to create little spikes in the custard after you add it to the tart. This custard is a richer variation on the Crema Pasticcera on page 88.

½ batch (250 grams) Pasta Frolla (page 67)

2 pears, peeled, cored, and cut into small dice

4 egg yolks

½ cup plus 2 tablespoons (120 grams) sugar

2 tablespoons (15 grams) potato starch

⅔ cup (160 grams) whole milk

⅓ cup (80 grams) heavy cream

Finely grated zest of 1 lemon

Blackberries for garnish

Pear slices for garnish

PREHEAT the oven to 325°F (160°C).

REMOVE the dough from the plastic wrap and dust it with flour. Lightly dust a flat work surface with flour and roll out the dough to a ¼- to ⅛-inch (about ½-centimeter) thickness and use it to line a 9-inch (23-centimeter) round cake pan or springform pan, pressing it into the bottom and sides. Scatter the diced pears in an even layer over the crust and set aside.

FOR the custard, in a small bowl, whisk together the egg yolks, sugar, and potato starch until the mixture is smooth and has reached the ribbon stage. Combine the milk and cream in a pot and heat over low heat until it just begins to boil. Gradually add the egg yolk mixture, whisking constantly. Continue to whisk over low heat until the mixture comes to a rolling boil. Stir in the lemon zest and immediately remove from the heat.

POUR the custard over the pears in the tart shell. Bake in the preheated oven until both crust and custard are browned, about 25 minutes. Cool the tart in the pan before serving. Garnish with a few blackberries and slices of pear.

CROSTATA ALLA FRUTTA

FRESH FRUIT TART

Makes one 9-inch (23-centimeter) tart, 8 to 10 servings

This classic tart will work with any fresh summer fruit. Mixed berries are lovely, but so are sliced peaches, plums, or apricots. Slice strawberries if using, but leave raspberries, blueberries, and blackberries whole. Sprinkle with confectioners' sugar just before serving if desired. Since the pasta frolla is blind-baked (baked without a filling), both it and the pastry cream can be prepared in advance, making it easy to assemble the tart shortly before you plan to serve it.

½ batch (250 grams) Pasta Frolla (opposite)

1 cup (250 grams) Crema Pasticcera (page 88)

3 cups (300 grams) mixed berries

PREHEAT the oven to 325°F (160°C). Roll the dough ¼ inch (⅔ centimeter) thick and about 10 inches (25 centimeters) in diameter and use it to line the bottom and sides of a 9-inch (23-centimeter) tart pan with a removable bottom. Prick the shell all over with a fork. Bake the shell until the pastry is dry and golden, 20 to 25 minutes. Let the shell cool in the pan on a rack for 10 minutes, then unmold and cool the unmolded shell on the rack on the tart pan bottom until completely cooled.

TO assemble the tart, spread the pastry cream in an even layer in the cooked tart shell. Arrange the berries in concentric circles on top. Serve at cool room temperature.

PASTA FROLLA
SHORTCRUST PASTRY

Makes about 1¼ pounds (585 grams) dough, enough for 2 single-crust tarts,
1 double-crust tart, or 1 lattice-crust tart

Pasta frolla is a tender short-crust pastry that is used for many different desserts in Italy. It can be used to make a single-crust tart, a double-crust tart, or a lattice-crust tart. You can also roll out pasta frolla, cut it into shapes, and bake it at 350°F (180°C) to make cookies. Refrigerate the dough up to 3 days or freeze up to 1 month. Thaw to room temperature before using.

2 cups (250 grams) unbleached all-purpose flour

1 stick plus 4 tablespoons (175 grams) unsalted butter, at room temperature, cut into chunks (see Note)

½ cup (100 grams) sugar

1 large egg

Finely grated zest of 1 lemon

PLACE the flour on a work surface (or in a bowl) and form a well. Place the butter in the well. Work in the butter until it forms large chunks. Add the sugar and continue to combine into a shaggy dough. Add the egg and knead until smooth. Add the finely grated lemon zest and knead to combine. Use a bench scraper to collect all the dough. Shape it into a log or two logs (or disks) and wrap in plastic wrap. Refrigerate the dough you will be using immediately for at least 1 hour and up to 3 days. Freeze for longer storage.

TO roll out pasta frolla, work on a lightly floured work surface, turning the dough frequently to maintain a circular shape. When you have rolled out the dough as desired, transfer it to the pan and press it into the bottom and sides of the pan. Don't worry if it tears a little—it is easily fixed. Trim the top of the crust, and use any scraps to patch tears or any spots that look too thin. Roll the remaining scraps into a thin rope. Use that rope to build a sturdy rim around the edge. (This is especially crucial if you are creating a lattice top for the tart; see pages 76–77 for instructions.)

A NOTE ABOUT THE BUTTER: *The butter for pasta frolla should be room temperature. In other words, it should be cold to the touch, but not so soft that it loses its shape. An hour or so out of the refrigerator at room temperature should be enough to get it ready.*

Come Fare la Pasta Frolla

LA FRUTTA
COME DOLCE

Despite our roster of incredible sweets in Italy, plain fruit is the most common dessert. Every meal at home ends with the fruit bowl brought to the table. Diners pick a piece, then peel it and eat it. This is a pleasant way to extend the meal, as well as a method for satisfying your sweet tooth. Sometimes, though, we crave a little something extra—fruit that is more than just fruit. That doesn't have to be an elaborate cake. It doesn't even have to mean turning on the oven. But we do like to incorporate these fruit-plus ideas into our regular meals.

PESCHE AL VINO BIANCO Slice ripe peeled and pitted peaches and drop them into a bowl. Sprinkle on a small amount of sugar (especially if the peaches aren't perfectly ripe). Add enough white wine to cover them and then refrigerate for at least 1 hour. Serve chilled.

CILIEGE AL VINO ROSSO Combine red wine, a little sugar, a sprinkling of ground cinnamon, some honey, and lemon juice in a pot. Bring to a boil and add cherries (pitted or not) and simmer over low heat for about 15 minutes. Let the cherries cool in the cooking liquid, then transfer them to a jar and add enough of the cooled liquid to cover completely. Place a lemon slice on top of the jar before sealing. Serve cold.

MACEDONIA This dish gets its name from the multiethnic heritage of the republic. Dice peeled ripe fruit of all kinds and toss with a sprinkling of sugar and a healthy dose of lemon juice. Store in the refrigerator. Serve with a dollop of whipped cream and a scattering of flaked almonds.

COMPOSTA DI FRUTTA INVERNALE Dice peeled apples and pears and combine them in a pot with diced prunes, dried apricots, raisins, and dried figs. Add water just to cover, then add a cinnamon stick. Simmer over low heat for 45 minutes until fruit is soft. Serve warm or chilled.

COMPOSTA DI FRUTTA ESTIVA Pit and dice nectarines, apricots, and plums. Melt a little butter in a saucepan and toss the diced fruit over medium heat until combined and softened, just a couple of minutes, then sprinkle on a little sugar and drizzle in a small amount of wine. Simmer until the wine has almost completely evaporated, about 8 minutes. Chill and serve cold on its own or over ice cream.

SEASONAL FRUIT

Apples and pears are typically picked in autumn, though they are good keepers and available year-round. Table grapes and wine grapes are also harvested in autumn, as are bright orange persimmons. Spring and summer herald the arrival of stone fruits (pears, peaches, plums, apricots) and berries. Citrus, which grows in the South, is best in winter. The lemons that grow on the island of Procida off the coast of Napoli are so sweet that they are served raw in salad. Prickly pears—ranging in color from yellow to shocking pink—are plucked (carefully!) from cactuses in the South, particularly on Sicilia, but they originated in Mexico. Fluorescent pomegranates have flourished all over the boot since ancient times.

FILLINGS AND TOPPINGS

Since fruit is typically soft, and grows softer when very ripe or cooked, topping it with a little crunch is never a bad idea. Almonds (and the amaretti cookies made with them) have a natural affinity with stone fruits and cherries. Honey marries well with almost anything, especially apples and pears. Peaches sliced and dropped into either red wine or white wine are a late-summer tradition.

TORTA AL GRANO SARACENO E MIRTILLI

BUCKWHEAT CAKE WITH BLUEBERRY JAM

Makes one 9-inch (23-centimeter) cake, about 12 servings   *Trentino–Alto Adige*

Buckwheat imparts an earthy flavor that always works well with fruit preserves. To acheive the soft consistency you are looking for, try to deflate the whipped egg whites as little as possible when you are incorporating them.

2 sticks plus 5 tablespoons (300 grams) unsalted butter, at room temperature, plus more for the pan

1½ cups (300 grams) sugar

6 large eggs, separated

2½ cups (300 grams) buckwheat flour

2½ teaspoons (10 grams) baking powder

1¼ cups (400 grams) blueberry jam

Confectioners' sugar for dusting

PREHEAT the oven to 350°F (180°C). Butter two 9-inch (23-centimeter) cake pans and set aside.

WITH a mixer, beat the butter with 1 cup (200 grams) of sugar. Add the egg yolks and beat until combined. In a clean bowl and with clean beaters, beat the egg whites until they form soft peaks, then add the remaining ½ cup (100 grams) sugar and beat to stiff peaks. Stir the flour and baking powder into the butter and yolk mixture until combined. With a spatula, fold in the whipped egg whites.

TRANSFER to the prepared pans and bake in the preheated oven until the tops spring back and a tester emerges clean, about 20 minutes. Cool completely on a rack.

WHEN the layers are completely cooled, invert them onto a rack one at a time, then turn them right side up and trim the tops level, if necessary. Place one layer on a cake plate, flat (bottom) side down, and spread the blueberry jam on top of it. Invert the second layer on top so that the flat (bottom) side is facing up. Dust with confectioners' sugar just before serving.

CONSERVE DI FRUTTA

Fresh fruit is preserved in a variety of different ways so that it can be enjoyed year-round. These concoctions are used in desserts such as jam tarts, but they are also wonderful as toppings for ice cream and simple spoon sweets.

MARMELLATA Made of citrus, marmellata consists of at least 20 percent fruit.

CONFETTURA Confettura is a jam made with any non-citrus fruit and consists of at least 35 percent fruit. A confettura is pulpy, not smooth.

CONFETTURA EXTRA The "extra" in the name refers to the amount of fruit, which must reach at least 45 percent.

COMPOSTA Fruit spreads rely only on the fruit's natural sugars for sweetness.

CONSERVA These preserves are the chunkiest type of all and may contain either whole fruit (such as preserved cherries) or diced fruit.

GELATINA Jelly is made with fruit juice only, so it has none of the chunkiness of the other options. It also contains sugar and pectin.

FRUTTA SECCA Dried fruit such as prunes, sultana raisins, and dried apricots is available year-round and provides a chewy texture and welcome tart flavor to many baked goods. And it makes a great snack.

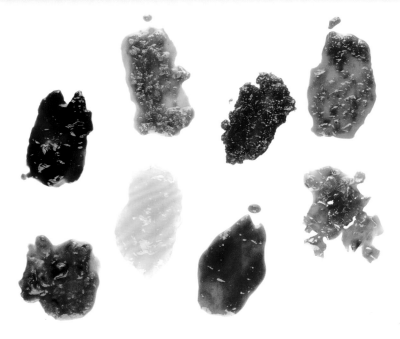

CROSTATA INTEGRALE ALLE FRAGOLE

STRAWBERRY JAM TART IN A WHOLE WHEAT CRUST

Makes one 9-inch (23-centimeter) tart, 8 to 10 servings

A lattice-topped jam tart is a classic home-baked dessert in Italy—the reward for having taken the time to put up jam and preserves in the warmer months. A whole wheat crust makes this one rustic and satisfying. The dough for this recipe is a whole wheat variation on Pasta Frolla (page 67).

1¼ cups (125 grams) whole wheat flour

1¼ cups (125 grams) pastry flour

1 teaspoon (3 grams) baking powder

¼ teaspoon (2 grams) salt

1 stick plus 2 tablespoons (150 grams) unsalted butter, at room temperature, cut into pieces

¼ cup plus 2 tablespoons (75 grams) sugar

1 large egg, lightly beaten

1 cup (300 grams) strawberry jam

COMBINE the flours, baking powder, and salt and place on a work surface (or in a bowl) and form a well. Place the butter in the well. Work in the butter until it forms large chunks. Add the sugar and continue to combine into a shaggy dough. Add the egg and knead until smooth. Use a bench scraper to collect all the dough. Shape it into a log and wrap in plastic wrap.

PREHEAT the oven to 350°F (180°C).

RESERVE about one-third of the dough. (Refrigerate if your kitchen is very warm.) On a lightly floured surface, roll out the remaining dough ¼ inch (about ½ centimeter) thick. Line a 9-inch (23-centimeter) pie or tart pan with the dough, fitting it against the sides. Spread the strawberry jam in an even layer on the dough.

ROLL out the remaining dough and use it to create a lattice. (See pages 76–77.)

BAKE until the crust is golden, about 30 minutes. Cool before serving.

Come Fare la Crostata con Reticolo

A LATTICE CRUST ON TOP OF A TART is a pretty touch that is not difficult to achieve in the least. It forms diamonds with the filling peeking through. If you plan to create a lattice for your tart, you will need more dough than if you were just making a single-crust tart. The lattice requires about half as much dough as the bottom crust. The instructions below are for creating a lattice crust in a round pie or tart pan, but you can make a lattice crust in a square or rectangular pan as well.

This system is not fussy or complicated, but if you're in a hurry and don't want to bother with a ruler, you can also roll the lattice dough into thin ropes—about the width of a pencil—and use those to create a lattice on top of the tart.

Roll out the bottom crust, retaining about one-half of the dough for the lattice. Be sure that the rim of the bottom crust is sturdy. If necessary, roll a thin rope of dough and attach it around the rim. Fill the tart.

Roll out the dough for the lattice about ¼ inch (½ centimeter) thick. Use a ruler to mark strips of ½ to 1 inch (1¼ to 2½ centimeters). Cut the strips using a knife or pastry cutter.

Place one set of strips parallel to each other on top of the tart, pinching them to seal them to the rim.

Place the remaining strips parallel to each other and at a 45-degree angle to the first set of strips. Trim any excess dough.

After trimming any excess dough, pinch the ends of the lattice strips against the perimeter of the dough to adhere.

77

STRUDEL DI MELE

APPLE STRUDEL

Makes one 12-inch (30-centimeter) strudel, 6 to 8 servings   *Trentino–Alto Adige*

Though you may associate strudel more closely with Austria than with Italy, strudel in a puff pastry case is the signature dessert of the Trentino–Alto Adige region, which was part of the Austro-Hungarian empire until 1919.

DOUGH AND FINISHING

14 ounces (400 grams) Pasta Sfoglia (page 52) or 2 sheets store-bought puff pastry

1 large egg, lightly beaten

FILLING

½ cup (100 grams) sugar

3 tablespoons (43 grams) unsalted butter

2 pounds (900 grams) apples, peeled, cored, and cut into ½-inch (1¼-centimeter) dice

¾ cup (70 grams) coarse breadcrumbs

2 Amaretti cookies (page 20 or store-bought), finely crushed

Finely grated zest of 1 lemon

ON a piece of parchment paper, roll out homemade puff pastry to a rectangle about ¼ inch (⅔ centimeter) thick and about 14 × 18-inches (36 × 46-centimeters) wide, or overlap the sheets slightly, press gently to seal them together, and trim to the correct size. Use the parchment to slide the dough onto a baking sheet or jelly-roll pan and refrigerate.

PREHEAT the oven to 350°F (180°C).

FOR THE FILLING, in a large sauté pan, combine the sugar and butter. Bring the mixture to a low boil over medium heat and stir until the sugar dissolves, about 1 minute. Add the apples and cook, stirring to coat, about 2 minutes. Remove from the heat and add the bread-crumbs, cookie crumbs, and lemon zest; stir well to combine.

TRANSFER the chilled dough with the parchment to a work surface. Mound the filling in a 12 × 3-inch (30 × 8-centimeter) strip, about 2 inches (5 centimeters) up from the bottom edge of the dough, leaving a 2½-inch (6-centimeter) border of dough on either end of the filling at the short ends; brush the dough with the egg. (Reserve egg wash.) Fold in the two short ends of the dough to cover the filling. From the bottom edge, roll up the strudel using the parchment paper and ending with the strudel seam-side down. Roll onto a baking sheet. Brush the outside of the dough with the egg wash.

BAKE in the preheated oven, rotating the pan once halfway through, until the strudel is evenly golden in color, about 40 minutes. Remove the strudel from the oven and allow it to cool on the pan on the rack until just warm, at least 30 minutes.

PASTICCERIA E DOLCETTI

The full range of Italian creativity and art are expressed through the country's fanciful pastries and delicate confections.

BABÀ AL RHUM

RUM BABAS

Makes 1 dozen pastries   *Campania*

Yeast-leavened babà are a specialty of Napoli. Serve a dollop of pastry cream or whipped cream (see pages 88–89) on top of each. At Eataly we make our babà in shaped molds, but you can use any type of ramekin or even a muffin tin with large indentations. These actually benefit from being made in advance—more soaking time translates into boozier babà. If you have active dry yeast rather than instant yeast on hand, dissolve it in a couple of tablespoons of warm water before adding.

CAKES

3¾ cups (450 grams) unbleached all-purpose flour, plus more for pan

½ cup (100 grams) sugar

2¼ teaspoons (1 envelope/ 7 grams) instant yeast

8 large eggs

2 sticks (230 grams) unsalted butter, softened, plus more for pan

2 teaspoons (10 grams) salt

SYRUP

1 cup (200 grams) sugar

½ cup (120 milliliters) dark rum

BUTTER and flour a 12-cup muffin pan or 12 babà pans and set aside.

IN the bowl of a stand mixer fitted with the dough hook, combine the flour, sugar, and yeast. Mix on low speed until incorporated.

RAISE the speed to medium and add the eggs one at a time, beating to incorporate between additions. When you have added all the eggs, beat the dough until thick and batter-like, about 10 minutes. Turn off the mixer and add 14 tablespoons (200 grams) of the softened butter and the salt. Beat on high speed until the dough pulls away from the sides of the bowl, about 10 minutes. The dough should be shiny and smooth.

REMOVE the dough from the mixing bowl. Butter your hands with the remaining 2 tablespoons (30 grams) softened butter. With buttered hands, divide the dough into 12 equal portions. (A kitchen scale is useful for this.) Place each portion in one of the indentations in the prepared muffin pan or one of the babà pans, cover loosely with a towel, and allow to stand at room temperature until doubled in bulk, about 1 hour.

PREHEAT the oven to 325°F (160°C). Bake the cakes in the preheated oven until they are cooked through and a toothpick inserted in the center emerges clean, 20 to 25 minutes. Cool in the pan on a rack for 20 minutes. Remove the cakes from the pan and place them on the rack set over a baking sheet or jelly-roll pan.

FOR the syrup, in a small saucepan, bring 1 cup (240 millimeters) water and sugar to a boil and stir to dissolve the sugar. Lower the heat to an active simmer and cook for 15 minutes to form a simple syrup. Remove from heat, add the rum, and stir to mix. Allow to cool for 5 minutes.

POKE the tops of the cakes with a popsicle stick to form 8 to 10 slits in each. Spoon the syrup over the cakes and into the slits. Collect any syrup that drips onto the pan and spoon it over the cakes again, then repeat a third time. Serve at room temperature.

DELIZIE AL LIMONE

LEMON DELIGHTS

Makes 6 individual cakes   *Campania*

Sunny Campania is known for its lemons, which are especially sweet and juicy and are used to make both local limoncello liqueur and these brightly flavored lemon pastries. These little domes fill the cases of pastry shops all along the coast. You will need a silicone mold with six half-sphere cavities to make these. Each indentation should have a capacity of about 3½ ounces (100 milliliters), and the cavities should be about 2½ inches (6 centimeters) in diameter.

CAKES

2 large eggs

1 egg yolk

¼ cup plus 1 tablespoon (60 grams) sugar

⅓ cup (30 grams) pastry flour

3 tablespoons (30 grams) potato starch

Finely grated zest of 1 lemon

SYRUP

3 tablespoons (35 grams) sugar

⅓ cup (70 grams) limoncello

Zest of 1 lemon in strips

FOR the cakes, preheat the oven to 350°F (180°C). Beat the eggs, yolk, and sugar until thickened. Sift in the flour and starch and then add the zest and beat until the mixture is fluffy. Transfer the batter to 6 half-sphere silicone molds—it should fill them almost to the top—and bake in the preheated oven until a tester inserted in the center emerges clean, about 20 minutes. Cool in the molds on a rack for about 10 minutes, then unmold and cool completely.

FOR the syrup, whisk together 3 tablespoons (35 millimeters) water, the sugar, limoncello, and lemon zest in a saucepan until the sugar has dissolved, bring to a boil, and simmer until reduced slightly, about 3 minutes. Strain out and discard the zest and allow the syrup to cool.

FOR THE FILLING: Combine the egg yolks and ⅓ cup (50 grams) of the sugar in a small saucepan and whisk until light in color and thickened. Whisk in the lemon juice and zest and place over medium heat. Cook, whisking constantly, until the mixture reaches the consistency of mayonnaise. Remove from the heat. Whisk in the butter one piece at a time. Transfer to a small bowl, cover with plastic wrap pressed against the surface, and refrigerate until cool. Whip the heavy cream and remaining 2 tablespoons sugar to stiff peaks. Refrigerate until ready to use.

FILLING AND FINISHING

3 egg yolks

⅓ cup plus 2 tablespoons (70 grams) sugar

⅓ cup (70 milliliters) freshly squeezed lemon juice

Finely grated zest of 1 lemon

5 tablespoons (70 grams) unsalted butter, cut into 20 pieces

1½ cups (360 grams) heavy cream

1 cup (250 grams) Crema Pasticcera (page 88)

TO assemble the cakes, fold together the lemon curd filling and the crema pasticcera. Turn over a cake, flat side up, and use a pastry bag to pipe as much of this mixture as possible into the center. Repeat with each dome. You will have filling left over. Transfer the filled cakes to a large shallow bowl where they fit in a single layer and pour the syrup over them. Brush the cakes with the syrup to be sure they are completely coated. Transfer the filled and syrup-coated cakes to the freezer and chill until firm, about 1 hour. When the cakes are firm, place them on individual serving plates or all together on a platter. Fold together the leftover lemon cream with the whipped cream and use this mixture to decorate the outside of the cakes (piping rosettes is the traditional way). Refrigerate until ready to serve.

UNA PASTICCERIA ITALIANA

IF YOU HAVE EVER BEEN IN ITALY ON A SUNDAY, you have likely noticed an interesting phenomenon: Dozens of people rushing through the streets carrying what appear to be beautifully wrapped gifts.

Holidays like Easter and Christmas come but once a year, but Sunday rolls around every week, and in Italy even in these hectic modern times, we celebrate every Sunday with a big family meal. We gather together, usually in our homes, and enjoy a long and leisurely lunch (as well as a soccer game). And if you are invited to someone's house for Sunday lunch—even a close relative—there is really only one gift to bring: a tray of pastries from a pastry shop.

An Italian *pasticceria* is a beautiful sight and always has a large glass case filled with tray after tray of tartlets, cream puffs, cannoli, and more. (It likely also has a bar and some tables where you can enjoy an espresso and a pastry on-site.) The pastry counters inside our stores are arranged the same way, in accordance with the Italian proverb *Anche l'occhio vuole la sua parte*, which roughly translates as "The eye needs to be fed as well," meaning that the aesthetics of food are as important as taste. Looking at the array of treats available, you can't help but be inspired—not to mention hungry (see photos pages 86–87).

In Italy, you select the pastries you want (we suggest multiples of a few favorites so there's no fighting over who gets the lone *meringata*) and the person behind the counter arranges them on a metallic cardboard tray, then wraps the tray in pretty paper printed with the pastry shop's name and ties the whole package with a ribbon. If you really can't wait, buy an extra pastry for yourself and enjoy it for breakfast with a coffee. Now you just have to be sure to arrive at your destination on time!

From top to bottom: Supir, Strawberry Mousse, Cioccolato, Pistachio Choux

From left to right: Espresso Semifreddo, Cocco Bello, Terracotta

Mini Rum Babàs

From top to bottom: Chocolate Choux, Chantilly Choux

CREMA PASTICCERA

PASTRY CREAM

Makes about 2 cups (500 grams) pastry cream

If you know how to make a basic pastry cream, a world of desserts opens up to you. We use pastry cream in many preparations in Italy, from tarts to cakes and pastries. We also sometimes eat it as a custard. Pastry cream can be flavored easily: it can have cocoa powder folded into it to make a chocolate version, or it can have a strip of lemon zest simmered with the milk, or you can stir a few drops of vanilla extract or any other extract into the finished cream. The method below should prevent any lumps from forming, but if they do, simply force the cream through a sieve. Pastry cream keeps in the refrigerator for a few days, but it can get overly thick. Whisk in a few spoonfuls of milk to loosen it if necessary. In Italy we tend to thicken creams like this one with cornstarch, while in the United States flour is preferred. At Eataly in the U.S. we use a little of both to strike a happy medium, but if you have a preference you can use all flour or all starch.

1 large egg

1 egg yolk

½ cup (100 grams) sugar

2 tablespoons (15 grams) pastry flour or unbleached all-purpose flour

2 tablespoons (20 grams) cornstarch

1⅓ cups (300 grams) whole milk

IN a small bowl, whisk together the egg, yolk, and sugar until they are pale yellow. Whisk in the flour and cornstarch until smooth and set aside. Place the milk in a pot and set over low heat. When the first bubbles appear, whisk about ¼ cup of the hot milk into the egg mixture, then add the egg mixture to the pot with the milk and cook, whisking constantly, until it begins to boil. It will thicken in 30 seconds to 1 minute. Transfer to a bowl, cover with plastic wrap, resting the wrap against the surface of the cream, and refrigerate until chilled.

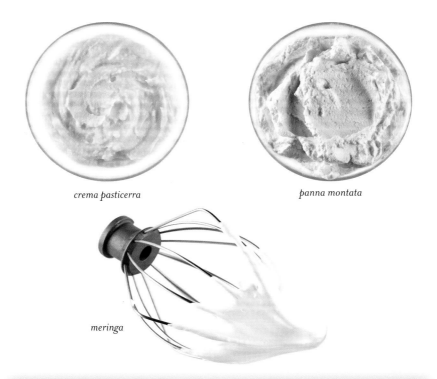

crema pasticerra

panna montata

meringa

PANNA MONTATA Soft, billowy whipped cream (also known as crema Chantilly when it is flavored with vanilla and sweetened) is used in many Italian desserts, either for finishing or as a filling. It is possible to whip cream by hand, but it takes a lot of effort. Use the biggest whisk you've got and work it back and forth in a Z shape. Or rely on a stand or hand-held mixer, which accomplishes the task in a flash. Cream will whip to greater volume if it is cold, and chilling the beaters and bowl also helps. We like to whip cream to soft peaks (slightly thickened, but still a little droopy), then add the sugar and continue whipping until it forms a firm peak that stands up when you lift the beater.

MERINGA Egg whites are whipped to create meringue the same way that cream is whipped, though egg whites whip better when slightly warm or at room temperature. Egg whites will never whip if there is a trace of fat in the bowl, so always scrupulously clean the bowl and beaters.

CREMA DIPLOMATICA Diplomat cream (which is used in the Trancetti Diplomatici on page 90) is simply whipped cream and pastry cream folded together. Always use a rubber spatula to fold the cream together gently, deflating it as little as possible.

TRANCETTI DIPLOMATICI
PASTRY SQUARES WITH DIPLOMAT CREAM

Makes 2 dozen 2-inch (5-centimeter) square pastries

A diplomatico represents the best of all worlds: crisp puff pastry, soft rum-soaked sponge cake, smooth cream filling. This isn't difficult to make, but it does have a number of elements, all of which should be completely cooled when you assemble the dessert. You will need one half of a rectangular Pan di Spagna layer (page 42) to assemble this dessert. If you know you are going to make this, you can make a small rectangle in a quarter-sheet pan (9 × 13-inches/ 23 × 33-centimeters) with half of the batter and make another round or rectangular layer to freeze, or simply make a full-size rectangular layer and cut it in half. If you prefer a round dessert that you can cut into wedges, use half of a round layer of Pan di Spagna cut horizontally to ¾ inch (2 centimeters) high and two 9-inch (23-centimeter) disks of puff pastry as for the Millefoglie on page 151.

PASTRY AND CAKE

½ pound (240 grams) Pasta Sfoglia (page 52) or 2 sheets store-bought puff pastry, rolled very thin and 9 × 13-inches (23 × 33-entimeters)

¼ cup (50 grams) sugar

1 (9 × 13 × ¾-inch/ 23 × 33 × 2-centimeter) Pan di Spagna layer

FILLING AND FINISHING

1¼ cups (300 grams) heavy cream

2 cups (500 grams) Crema Pasticcera (page 88)

3 tablespoons (25 grams) cocoa powder

Confectioners' sugar for dusting

IF using homemade puff pastry, roll the sheets out on parchment paper to make two rectangles. (It is easier to cut the dough in half and work with one half at a time.) Each should be less than ¹⁄₁₀ inch (2 millimeters) thick and at least 9 × 13-inches (23 × 33-centimeters) in size. (You will trim the edges later.) Transfer the dough on the parchment to the baking sheets or jelly-roll pans and refrigerate for 8 hours to prevent shrinking.

PREHEAT the oven to 300°F (150°F). Prick the puff pastry all over with a fork, spray with water, and sprinkle with the sugar. Bake at 300°F (150°F) for 10 minutes, then turn up the oven temperature to 350°F (180°C) and bake until golden brown and crisp, about 5 additional minutes. (Poke again with a fork if the pastry is puffing a lot in the oven.) Remove and allow to cool completely.

FOR the filling, whip the cream to stiff peaks and fold it into the crema pasticcera. Divide this mixture in half. Leave one half as is and sift the cocoa powder over the other half, then fold the cocoa in until combined. For the syrup, whisk together ½ cup (100 milliliters) water

SYRUP

½ cup (100 grams) sugar

1 tablespoon (20 milliliters) rum

and the sugar in a saucepan until the sugar has dissolved, then bring to a boil and simmer for 3 minutes, whisking frequently. Remove from the heat and stir in the rum. Set aside to cool.

TO ASSEMBLE, place the less-flat rectangle of puff pastry on a large platter or on the bottom of a quarter-sheet pan. (You can place a piece of parchment under the puff pastry to make it easier to get the assembled dessert out of the pan, and overturning the pan will help; when you're ready to slide the assembled dessert onto the work surface.) Spread the cocoa powder filling on top in an even layer. Arrange the cake in an even layer to cover the surface and brush it all over with the rum syrup, using all of the syrup. Spread the filling without the cocoa powder in an even layer on top of the cake. Place the second (flatter) puff pastry rectangle on top. Wrap the assembled dessert in plastic and freeze for at least 1 hour. (It will cut much more neatly when frozen.) Remove from the freezer, slide onto a cutting board or work surface, and trim with a serrated knife, cleaning the knife between cuts, to make an 8 by 12-inch (20 by 30-centimeter) rectangle with neatly squared off sides. Mark with a ruler and slice into squares, again cleaning the knife between cuts to avoid dragging chocolate cream across the rest of the cake. Allow the squares to thaw to room temperature. Dust individual slices with confectioners' sugar before serving.

CANNOLI SICILIANI

SICILIAN CANNOLI

Makes 3 to 4 dozen small cannoli   *Sicilia*

We like to make small cannoli at Eataly, so count on two of these per serving. You will need a set of cannoli tubes to make these (see photos, pages 94–95).

SHELLS

1²⁄₃ cups (200 grams) unbleached all-purpose flour

1 tablespoon (20 grams) unsalted butter

2 tablespoons (20 grams) sugar

1 tablespoon (80 grams) Marsala wine

1 teaspoon (5 grams) freshly squeezed lemon juice

1 teaspoon (5 grams) white vinegar

¼ teaspoon (2 grams) salt

1 egg yolk, lightly beaten

Vegetable oil for frying

FILLING

¾ cup plus 2 tablespoons (180 grams) sugar

2 cups (500 grams) sheep's milk ricotta, drained

½ cup (75 grams) chocolate chips or ½ cup (40 grams) diced candied orange peel (page 103)

FOR the shells, mix all the ingredients except the egg yolk and frying oil in a large bowl and knead in the bowl until the dough is stiff and smooth. Cover and refrigerate until firm, about 2 hours.

ON a lightly floured surface, roll the dough to a thickness of 2 millimeters (¹⁄₁₂ inch), then transfer to a baking sheet and refrigerate for at least 2 hours. Using a round 3-inch (8-centimeter) cookie cutter, cut out disks of dough. Dab egg yolk at one end of a disk and wrap the disk around a cannoli tube, overlapping the ends to form a tube and pressing lightly to seal. Repeat with as many tubes as you have.

FILL a heavy pot with high sides with several inches of vegetable oil for frying. Clip a candy thermometer to the side and heat the oil to 350°F (180°C). Line the baking sheets or jelly-roll pans with paper towels. Carefully lower the shells, still wrapped around the tubes, into the oil (don't crowd the pan) and fry until dark golden brown, 2 to 3 minutes. Remove with tongs and place on the paper towel–lined pan to drain. When the fried shells have cooled enough to touch, slip out the tubes (use caution as the metal may still be hot) and repeat with the remaining dough disks. The shells can be made up to one day in advance and allowed to rest at room temperature, unfilled and uncovered.

THE day before serving the cannoli, stir the sugar into the drained ricotta until smooth. Fold in the chocolate chips. Let the mixture rest in the refrigerator overnight.

JUST before serving (never fill cannoli in advance or they will get soggy), use a pastry bag fitted with a smooth tip to pipe filling into each shell from both ends.

Come Fare le Cialde dei Cannoli

FUNGHETTI

LITTLE MUSHROOM PASTRIES

Makes 2 to 3 dozen small pastries

These little mushrooms are as much fun to look at as they are to eat. If you prefer, you can purchase excellent quality gianduia cream at Eataly and use that to fill these. In addition, you can lightly sprinkle the pastries with cocoa powder before baking if desired.

1 batch Pasticcini dough (page 98)

3½ ounces (100 grams) 70% dark chocolate

½ cup (50 grams) hazelnuts, skinned (page 24)

¼ cup (30 grams) cocoa powder

GIANDUIA CREAM

⅓ cup (50 grams) hazel-nuts, skinned (see page 24)

⅓ cup (75 grams) heavy cream

2 cups (500 grams) Crema Pasticcera (page 88)

1¾ ounces (50 grams) dark chocolate (70% cacao), melted and cooled

2 tablespoons (15 grams) cocoa powder

BEFORE making the dough, preheat the oven to 375°F (190°C). Line the baking sheets or jelly roll pans with parchment and set aside.

WHEN the dough is ready, brush the parchment on the pans lightly with water, then pipe the dough onto the prepared pans in two sets of shapes in equal numbers: strips about 2¼ inches (6 centimeters) long for the stems, and round cream puffs about 1½ inches (4 centimeters) in diameter for the caps. Leave a few inches between them on the pans, and pat down any points or peaks that form with a moistened fingertip. Bake until the pastry is golden brown and puffy, about 30 minutes. Cool on the pans on racks.

FOR THE GIANDUIA CREAM, pulse the hazelnuts to a paste in a food processor fitted with the metal blade. Whip the cream to stiff peaks. Fold the crema pasticcera and whipped cream together with a rubber spatula. Fold in the melted chocolate, hazelnut paste, and cocoa powder.

WHEN the pastries have cooled, melt the chocolate in the top of a double boiler. Grind the hazelnuts coarsely and spread on a plate. Transfer the gianduia cream to a pastry bag fitted with a small tip. Cut a slit in the flat side of each puff and each stem and fill. Then use a dab of melted chocolate on the bottom of each puff to attach a stem. Dip the ends of the stems in melted chocolate and then in the ground hazelnuts. You can dip the caps as well, if you like. Place completed pastries on a platter, dust with cocoa powder, and serve.

FILLING PASTRIES

YOU CAN FILL CREAM PUFFS AND OTHER SIMILAR PASTRIES in one of two ways. Either cut them in half horizontally with a serrated knife and pipe the filling on the bottom halves and top with the caps, or place the filling in a piping bag fitted with a small tip, cut a slit into the bottom of each pastry, insert the tip, and pipe filling into the center. The recipe on the following page makes 3 to 4 dozen small cream puffs that are 1½ to 2 inches in diameter. To fill them you will need about 1 tablespoon per puff, or 2 to 3 cups of filling (250 to 375 grams of pastry cream or 240 to 360 milliliters of cream sweetened with ¼ cup (50 grams) to 6 tablespoons (75 grams) sugar and whipped to stiff peaks, as cream more or less doubles when whipped) to fill by piping. If you are cutting the pastries in half horizontally you have a lot of leeway (you can pipe tall rosettes and have the caps teeter on top, or you can be more restrained), but will need at least the same amount. You can use Crema Pasticcera (page 88) or Crema Diplomatica or sweetened whipped cream (page 89) to fill choux pastries, or get creative and flavor the creams any way you like. You can also dip the exteriors of pastries in melted chocolate or caramel, or sprinkle filled pastries with confectioners' sugar or cocoa powder. At Eataly we make something we call a tiramichoux: a chocolate-dipped cream puff filled with mascarpone cream. We are also partial to choux pastries filled with fresh raspberries and whipped cream. Larger puffs can be used to make profiteroles: fill with crema pasticcera, diplomat cream (crema pasticcera with an equal amount of sweetened whipped cream folded into it), or ice cream and then douse in chocolate ganache.

PASTICCINI

CREAM PUFFS

Makes 3 to 4 dozen small puffs

Choux paste is a marvel. When made properly it bakes up puffy and light. There are a few things to keep in mind, however. Never use your oven on the convection setting when baking choux puffs—they need as little air movement as possible. And don't open the oven during the first twenty minutes of baking or they'll collapse. Also, preheat the oven before you make the dough. It shouldn't sit around but be baked immediately. (See the previous page for filling and finishing suggestions and instructions.)

1 stick plus 6 tablespoons (200 grams) unsalted butter

1 tablespoon plus 1½ teaspoons (25 grams) salt

1¾ cups (210 grams) unbleached all-purpose flour

Up to 12 large eggs

PREHEAT the oven to 375°F (190°C). Line pans with parchment and set aside.

COMBINE the butter, ¾ cup plus 3 tablespoons (220 grams) water, and salt in a saucepan over medium heat and cook, stirring, until the butter has melted. Bring the mixture to a simmer, then add all of the flour and remove from the heat. Beat with a wooden spoon until the flour is completely combined into the liquid. Return the pan to the heat.

COOK, stirring constantly, until the dough begins to pull away from the sides of the pan and is quite thick, 2 to 5 minutes. Transfer the dough to a large bowl and let it cool for about 5 minutes. Lightly beat 5 of the eggs. With an electric mixer or working vigorously with a whisk, whisk in the 5 eggs. Continue to beat in the additional eggs, lightly beaten, one at a time, stirring to combine between additions. Add eggs until you have a glossy dough with a pipeable consistency. You may not need all of the eggs—the longer you cooked the dough on the stovetop, the fewer eggs you will need, as you are adding moisture back into the mixture.

LIGHTLY brush the parchment-lined pans with water. Transfer the dough to a pastry bag and pipe in desired shapes leaving 2 inches (5 centimeters) between them. Use a wet finger to gently smooth any peaks formed when you lift the piping bag. Bake until the pastry is golden brown and puffy, about 30 minutes, but this can vary widely depending on the size and shape. Cool completely before filling.

CANNONCINI

FILLED PUFF PASTRY TUBES

Makes 1 to 2 dozen 3-inch (7½ centimeter) pastries

You need a set of cone-shaped or tubular forms to make these. The ones used to make Cannoli Siciliani (page 93), which are about ¾ inch (2 centimeters) in diameter, work perfectly. You can improvise forms using heavy-duty aluminum foil. You will need about 3 cups filling, though the exact amount will depend on the diameter of the tubes used. Crema Pasticcera (page 88) flavored with strips of lemon zest simmered in the milk, or zabaione like the one on page 151 thickened with starch to make it firm enough to pipe, are traditional fillings. Store-bought puff pastry comes rolled out to about a ¼-inch thickness, so you won't have to do anything but cut it into strips.

1 pound (485 grams) Pasta Sfoglia (page 52) or 3 sheets store-bought puff pastry

2 egg yolks, beaten

½ cup (100 grams) sugar

3 cups (750 grams) Crema Pasticerra (page 88)

PREHEAT the oven to 350°F (180°C). Line jelly-roll pans or baking sheets with parchment paper and set aside. Divide homemade puff pastry into three batches. Refrigerate all but the batch you are working with. On a lightly floured surface, roll out the puff pastry to a rectangle about ¼ inch (⅔ centimeter) thick and 12 × 6-inches (30 × 15-centimeters) long. Cut into strips 1 inch (3 centimeter) wide and 12 inches (30 centimeters) long. Wrap one strip around a form in a spiral to make a cone or tube, pressing against the form lightly to seal and arranging the edges of the strip so that they touch, but do not overlap. Brush with egg yolk, sprinkle with sugar, and place the pastry on the form on the prepared pan. Repeat with remaining dough, refrigerating the forms that are ready. Bake on the forms until golden, about 20 minutes. Cool completely, then gently rotate to remove from the forms.

WHEN the pastries have cooled, transfer the crema pasticcera filling mixture to a pastry bag fitted with a small tip. Fill the pastries (working from both ends of the tubes) and serve immediately.

BACI

CHOCOLATE HAZELNUT KISSES

Makes 12 to 24 candies

You have probably tasted industrially made chocolate hazelnut kisses, and they're not bad, but the homemade kind are mind-blowingly good. You can use milk chocolate or white chocolate in place of the dark chocolate here for variety.

1⅓ cups (200 grams) hazelnuts, skinned (see page 24)

1 pound (450 grams) dark chocolate

1¼ cups (300 grams) gianduia spread

1 tablespoon (8 grams) cocoa powder

SET aside 30 whole hazelnuts. Chop the remaining hazelnuts in a food processor fitted with the metal blade. In a double boiler, melt a little more than 5 ounces (150 grams) of the dark chocolate. Add the chocolate hazelnut spread and stir to melt together and combine well. Remove from the heat and stir in the cocoa powder. Whisk until very smooth. Stir in the chopped hazelnuts.

TRANSFER the mixture to a casserole dish or pan lined with parchment paper. Chill in the refrigerator until cool but soft and malleable, about 1 hour.

REMOVE the mixture from the refrigerator. If it has grown too hard, let it sit for a few minutes at room temperature.

USING your hands, form the mixture into tiny balls (a little smaller than a golf ball) and place on a tray or baking sheet lined with parchment paper. Add 1 whole hazelnut on top of each ball. Refrigerate for 1 hour.

MELT the remaining 10½ ounces (300 grams) chocolate in a double boiler. Dip the base of each candy in the melted chocolate and place back on the parchment paper. Refrigerate until the chocolate hardens, 10 to 15 minutes.

PLACE a wire rack on a parchment-lined jelly-roll pan or baking sheet. Arrange the candies on the wire rack, then pour the remaining melted chocolate over them to coat. Refrigerate on the rack until firm, about 30 minutes.

VINO DA DESSERT

Wine is an important component in most Italian meals, but when celebrating a festive occasion we're even more likely to pair a special wine with dessert. Below are some of our favorite options.

PASSITO This is a sweet wine made with grapes that have been dried (either on or off the vine). It has an intensely sweet flavor and is sometimes referred to as "raisin wine" in English. Toscana's *vin santo*, de rigueur with Cantucci Toscani (page 18), is one famed example; *recioto*, which may be red or white, is another type. The *passito* from the island of Pantelleria, south of Sicilia, is justly renowned. Passito goes well with many Christmas and Easter specialties. It is also a good match with fruit tarts.

VINO LIQUOROSO A *vino liquoroso,* or fortified wine, has been enhanced with the addition of extra alcohol either during fermentation or upon completion. One of Italy's most famous examples is Marsala, which was created when Englishman John Woodhouse added aquavit as a preservative to some casks of wine before shipping them back to England. Fortified wines maintain their sweetness and last longer after opening because the addition of alcohol interrupts fermentation. Fruit desserts, such as Crostata di Pere con Crema Cotta (page 65), pair particularly well with fortified wines.

VINO AROMATIZZANTE An aromatized wine incorporates fruit, florals, spices, and other aromatics. *Barolo chinato* and *vermut* are two of Italy's more popular choices in this category. These are typically enjoyed after dessert.

VINO SPUMANTE Fizzy wines are a good companion to almost any dessert. Moscato d'Asti and Asti spumante from Piemonte are excellent white choices, and brachetto d'Acqui and Lambrusco are red sparkling wines that match well with both savory dishes and desserts. Crisp cookies such as Amaretti (page 20) are wonderful with them.

VINO FERMO DOLCE Most of the non-sparkling dessert wines in Italy are made from either Moscato or Malvasia grapes. Often you will find both sparkling and still versions of these. Smooth spoon desserts, such as Zabaione (page 151), not only sometimes incorporate these wines but also pair well with them.

PROSECCO Prosecco from the Veneto is Italy's reliable wine for celebrations and pairs just as well with appetizers as it does with dessert. Panettone and pandoro are almost always served with glasses of bubbly Prosecco. Prosecco may be *spumante* (sparkling) or *frizzante* (semi-sparkling). It is less carbonated and typically fruitier than its French cousin, Champagne.

CROCCANTE

NUT BRITTLE

Makes 12 to 24 pieces

You can make this nut brittle with any kind of nuts you like, or a combination of different kinds. Almonds (blanched and whole or slivered) and hazelnuts are favorites in Italy. The nuts can be left whole or chopped. A pinch of salt really makes this candy sing. We like to serve shards of this on a cookie plate at the end of a meal, but if you prefer you can cut it into neat strips or diamonds when it is still slightly warm rather than breaking it. It can also be crushed and used to decorate cakes and pastries.

Vegetable cooking spray for pan

1 cup (about 150 grams) whole blanched almonds, slivered almonds, skinned hazelnuts (see page 24), pine nuts, or other nuts of your choice

1 cup (200 grams) sugar

¼ cup (60 milliliters) water

LINE a baking sheet or jelly-roll pan with parchment paper and spray with the cooking spray. Chop the nuts if desired, or leave whole.

COMBINE the sugar and water in a pot (preferably one with a light-colored interior so you can judge the level of caramelization) and stir to combine thoroughly. Place over medium heat. Cook without stirring, but keep a close eye on it. The mixture should begin to color. If it is coloring unevenly, gently swirl the pan. When it is an amber color, about 10 minutes, stir in the nuts with a wooden spoon and stir constantly until the mixture turns very dark golden, 2 to 3 additional minutes. Pour it onto the prepared pan and smooth with an offset or silicone spatula. (You can also slide the parchment to a work surface, place another piece of parchment on top, and roll over the top with a rolling pin to make it even and smooth, then peel off the top piece of parchment.)

YOU can mark the candy into strips or any other shape while it is still warm using a butter knife, or wait for it to harden completely and break it into irregular shards.

SCORZETTE DI ARANCIA CANDITE

CANDIED ORANGE PEEL

Makes 2 to 3 cups (about 150 grams) candied orange peel strips

From December through April, bright, juicy oranges flood our market. As you incorporate citrus into your favorite dish (or drink!), don't forget about the peel! An excellent garnish, candied citrus peel is a treat on its own as a sweet finish to a meal; dipped in melted dark chocolate and then air-dried; or served with ricotta, honey, and toasted almonds. This recipe calls for oranges, but you can also candy the peels of grapefruit and lemons. Just don't stir the peels while they're cooking—the sugar will crystallize.

6 thick-skinned Valencia oranges

4½ cups (900 grams) sugar

CUT the tops and bottoms off of the fruit. Lightly score each orange into quarters, but do not cut into it. Peel off the skin and the pith of the fruit in large pieces. Cut the peel into ¼-inch (5-millimeter) strips.

PLACE the peel in a pot with just enough cold water to cover it, and bring to a boil over high heat. Pour out the water and repeat twice more. Heat the sugar and ½ cup (120 milliliters) water over high heat and simmer until the sugar has dissolved, 8 to 9 minutes. Add the peels and simmer gently without stirring until the peels become translucent, about 45 minutes. Spread the peels on a wire rack and allow to cool completely.

DOLCI DELLE FESTE

Every holiday has its own dessert,
and dessert makes any occasion a celebration.

FRITTELLE DI RICOTTA

RICOTTA FRITTERS

Makes 4 to 6 dozen fritters

Incorporating ricotta results in cloudlike fritters with a tender texture.

2 cups (500 grams) cow's milk ricotta, drained

⅓ cup (60 grams) sugar

3 large eggs

2 cups (200 grams) pastry flour

2 teaspoons (10 grams) baking powder

1 teaspoon (5 grams) salt

Vegetable oil for frying

Confectioners' sugar for sprinkling

IN a large bowl, combine the ricotta, sugar, and eggs. Sift the flour, baking powder, and salt together and then fold the dry ingredients into the ricotta mixture using a rubber spatula (or a stand mixer fitted with the paddle attachment). Cover and refrigerate for 1 hour.

LINE a baking sheet with paper towels. Fill a Dutch oven or stockpot with several inches of oil. Clip a candy thermometer to the pot, and place over medium heat. Bring the oil to 325°F (165°C) and regulate the heat to keep it at that temperature as you fry the dough.

USE a very small gelato scoop to scoop the batter into balls about the size of a golf ball and drop them into the oil, working in batches to keep from crowding the pan. Fry the fritters until dark brown, 6 to 7 minutes. As they are ready, remove them with a slotted spoon or skimmer and transfer to the prepared baking sheet to drain briefly. Dust with confectioners' sugar and serve warm or at room temperature.

CARNEVALE FRITTERS

The recipe on page 106 provides basic instructions for making one type of fritter for Carnevale, but naturally, each area of Italy makes them slightly differently. Some are flat, crispy ribbons; others are puffy doughnuts. There are also varying names for the fritters in different places. Whatever you call them and however they are made, they are delicious.

BUGIE *Piemonte* These "lies" are thin ribbons of dough made using a pasta machine or rolling pin, then fried until crispy; bugie often have melted butter and extra egg yolks in the dough.

CASTAGNOLE *Veneto, Liguria, Emilia-Romagna, Le Marche, Lazio* Literally "firecrackers," these balls of dough are usually topped with powdered sugar but sometimes drizzled with honey instead; castagnole may also be baked.

CENCI *Toscana* Very similar to bugie. Rolled thin and cut with a fluted pastry wheel for notched edges.

CHIACCHIERE *Lombardia* "Chatter" fritters are round and small in size.

FAVETTE *Veneto* These "little fava beans" are virtually identical to castagnole but tend to be smaller in size.

FRAPPE *Lazio* Like cenci, these are rolled thin and cut with a fluted pastry wheel, but the strips of dough are usually twisted once or twice before frying.

TORTELLI *Lombardia* These are round fritters made by dropping spoonfuls of batter into the hot oil. The batter is rather liquid, resulting in lots of big, airy holes. Tortelli are often filled with pastry cream.

ZEPPOLE *Umbria, Marche, Sardegna* Zeppole may be round or oval fritters, but the dough may also be shaped into crescents or rings. The dough often includes anise liqueur.

Frittelle di Ricotta

Castagnole

Bugie

PANI NATALIZI CHRISTMAS BREAD

PANNETTONE: PRETTILY WRAPPED AND RIBBON-TIED. Several versions of the eggy sweet bread dotted with dried fruit and candied citrus peel are found for sale all over Italy (and all over Eataly) during the Christmas season. Though panettone originated in Milano, it is now enjoyed everywhere. Interestingly, panettone (and its cousin, pandoro) is rarely if ever made at home. Panettone requires a long, slow rise and special pans, and the best versions are made with natural yeast, which can behave unpredictably. Panettone rises to a towering height and forms a beautiful brown dome that can easily collapse when it comes out of the oven. In other words, as enthusiastic as we are about home baking, panettone is a job best left to the professionals. In an unusual case of cross-regional migration in Italy, panettone and pandoro are sliced and served alongside local specialties (page 122) during the Christmas season.

THE ORIGINS OF PANETTONE ARE MURKY. We know it first appeared in Milano, but beyond that, the stories devolve into myth and legend that sound slightly dubious. The name is often presumed to be a variation of "pan di Toni," or Toni's bread. One legend claims a man created it for his unrequited love, Toni. Another has it that panettone, which is dark brown on top, was a burnt cake that was going to be tossed out until someone named Toni suggested serving it. We do know that Lombardia has a long history of breads made with honey and dried fruit.

PANDORO IS SIMILAR TO FRENCH BRIOCHE. From the city of Verona (the romantic setting for *Romeo and Juliet)* in the Veneto, this Christmas bread is always in the shape of an eight-pointed star. (It, too, is made in a special pan.) Pandoro means "golden bread." A Veronese baker patented pandoro in 1884.

THEN THERE ARE THE DENSER CHRISTMAS BREADS. From Cogne in Val d'Aosta comes mecoulin, a yeast-risen bread packed with dried fruit. In the city of Genova in the Liguria region, Christmas is celebrated with pandolce Genovese, a crumbly bread stuffed with dried fruit and nuts and flavored with fennel and coriander. And on the shores of Lago di Como pan mataloc is made with figs and hazelnuts. Locals also feast on miascia, a kind of cross between a bread pudding and a cake made by tearing pieces of stale bread, combining it with fresh and dried fruit and nuts, as well as eggs and milk, and then baking it in the oven until firm. The people of the Marche make pizza di Natale with figs, nuts, grated lemon and orange zest, and chocolate. Though it's called a pizza, it is shaped into a loaf. The pangiallo of Lazio is now associated with Christmas but was once made to show reverence for a Roman god of the sun, hence its yellow color.

ALL OF THESE BREADS ARE SWEET BUT NOT CLOYING. They lend themselves to projects—see page 116 for one fun thing to do with pandoro. Leftovers stay fresh for a surprisingly long time, but should your Christmas bread go stale, you can toast slices and serve them with a scoop of the Gelato alla Crema (page 136) or the Whipped Cream (page 89), or use slices past their prime to make a decadent bread pudding or trifle.

PANDORO CON CREMA AL MASCARPONE

PANDORO WITH MASCARPONE CREAM

Makes 1 cake, 8 to 12 servings

Eataly sells delicious artisanal versions of pandoro during the holiday season. Though this Christmas treat is rarely baked at home, you can make pandoro your own by slicing it up and reassembling it in a Christmas-tree shape with sweetened mascarpone filling and fruit between the layers (see photos opposite and following pages).

1 cup plus 1 tablespoon (250 grams) heavy cream

⅓ cup (70 grams) sugar

Juice of 1 lemon

1 cup (250 grams) mascarpone

1 (2.2-pound/1-kilogram) pandoro

2 pint baskets raspberries

1 pint basket blackberries

1 pint basket blueberries

Confectioners' sugar for dusting

WHIP the cream to soft peaks. Add the sugar and whip to stiff peaks, then fold the whipped cream and lemon juice into the mascarpone.

USE a serrated knife to cut the pandoro crosswise into six layers. The easiest way to do this is to first mark shallow cuts (use a ruler to make even marks) around the perimeter, turning the plate or stand with the cake on it, and then slice all the way through with a long knife using the marks as a guide.

PLACE the base of the pandoro on a serving plate. Spread a thin layer of the mascarpone mixture on it in an even layer and top with a few of the raspberries. Place the second layer of pandoro on top, turning it so that the spikes of the star shape are alternating with the spikes of the first layer. Repeat layers of cake, mascarpone cream, and fruit (using up one pint basket of raspberries) until you have placed the pointed top of the cake on top. Place raspberries, blackberries, and blueberries on the star points, then dust with confectioners' sugar and serve.

Come Zuccherare un Pandoro

Pandoro is almost always packaged with a little envelope of confectioners' sugar used to embellish the cake just before serving. We loved this ritual as kids, and we still enjoy it as adults. When it's time to sugar pandoro, everyone in the Eataly pastry kitchen wants a turn! Simply leave the pandoro in its cellophane wrapper, pour in the sugar, twist the top closed, and shake. Then push the cellophane down and transfer the pandoro to a platter or cake plate for serving.

DOLCI SPEZIATI

PANFORTE IS THE ITALIAN VERSION OF A CHRISTMAS FRUITCAKE: a layer of nuts, candied fruit, and spices served in thin wedges. Panforte has been made in the beautiful city of Siena (in Toscana) since the Middle Ages, when it was known as *panis fortis.* The original panforte was made with fresh fruit and honey and after being formed into a cake was allowed to ferment, which gave it a particularly acidic flavor. In 1550, while the city of Siena was under siege, a nun at the Monte Celso convent began making a tastier version of panforte to serve as rations that would fortify the combatants. She replaced the fresh fruit with candied fruit and added nuts and spices (including a sprinkling of black pepper) to make an early take on an energy bar. This new version of panforte became quite popular. Because it was heavily spiced, it was made by pharmacists, who at the time dosed out spices as medicine. The IGP (Indication of Geographic Protection) version of panforte di Siena is dense, ½ inch to 1¾ inches (14 to 45 millimeters) high, and round or rectangular in shape. Like torrone (page 127), panforte is often made with confectionery rice paper underneath and around the sides as it is very sticky. It requires a sharp knife for cutting.

THE VARIATIONS ON PANFORTE ARE ENDLESS. Sometimes known as panpepato, it may incorporate chili pepper in addition to or in place of black pepper. It may also contain cocoa powder or chopped chocolate, and sometimes the top is glazed with melted chocolate. The panpepato of Ferrara, in Emilia Romagna, is very similar but shaped into a dome rather than pressed into a level disk. While in Siena this sweet is closely associated with Christmas, it is popular for New Year's Day in Ferrara. Panforte Margherita was prepared for the queen when she visited Siena in 1879 to attend the Palio, a wild horse race around the city's main square that pits the city's seventeen *contrade*, or neighborhoods, against one another. That version is made with seventeen ingredients, including vanilla-flavored sugar in place of black pepper. It also contains candied pumpkin. Panforte nero is dark with spices; panforte bianco is sprinkled with confectioners' sugar.

BOLOGNA'S TAKE ON A SPICED CHRISTMAS FRUITCAKE is known as a Certosino, as it was invented by the city's Carthusian monks. Like panforte, this cake dates to the Middle Ages. In addition to spices, it traditionally contains candied fruit, chocolate, and honey and it is often baked in a ring. It, too, was originally the province of pharmacists because of the large amount of spices it contains. The top of a Certosino is decorated with candied fruit and it is glazed to a high sheen.

ZELTEN

FRUIT LOAF

Makes one 9 x 13-inch (23 x 33-centimeter) cake, 8 to 12 servings

Trentino—Alto Adige

Zelten is the signature Christmas dessert of Trentino–Alto Adige. Rich with dried fruit and nuts, it serves as a satisfying end to a holiday meal. Traditionally the top of the cake is decorated with nuts and dried fruit arranged in a decorative pattern. The name is similar to the German word *selten*, meaning "rarely," probably because the cake was traditionally prepared only once a year. This can also be made in a loaf pan or a round pan.

1 stick plus 1 tablespoon (125 grams) unsalted butter, softened, plus more for the pan

1¼ cups (250 grams) sugar

2 large eggs

6 cups (750 grams) all-purpose flour, plus more for flouring pan

2 tablespoons plus 2 teaspoons (32 grams) baking powder

2 cups (480 milliliters) milk

1 pinch salt

4 cups (400 grams) walnuts, chopped

1 cup (150 grams) dried figs, stemmed and chopped

1 cup (150 grams) raisins

1 cup (115 grams) diced candied citron

¼ cup (60 milliliters) brandy

Zest of 1 orange, grated

PREHEAT the oven to 350°F (180°C). Butter and flour a 9 × 13-inch (23 × 33-centimeter) rectangular pan and set aside.

BEAT the butter in a bowl for a few minutes until soft. Add the sugar and eggs and beat until thoroughly combined. Sift the flour and baking powder into the mixture and stir to combine. Stir in the milk and salt. Set aside some walnuts and dried figs for decorating the top. Stir in the remaining walnuts and figs, the raisins, the citron, the brandy, and the orange zest until combined. Mix for 10 minutes, then transfer the mixture to the prepared pan. There should be at least ⅓ inch (about 1 centimeter) between the surface of the batter and the top of the pan to allow room for the cake to rise. Decorate the surface with the reserved walnuts and figs.

BAKE in the preheated oven until the surface is golden and firm, about 40 minutes. Cool in the pan on a rack.

PARDULAS

OPEN-FACE RICOTTA AND SAFFRON PIES

Makes 1 to 2 dozen pastries

Pardulas from Sardegna feature two of the island's stellar products: saffron and creamy ricotta. With their crimped edges and golden color, they resemble little suns.

DOUGH

¾ cup plus 2 tablespoons (150 grams) semolina flour

1¼ cups (150 grams) unbleached all-purpose flour

2 egg whites

1 teaspoon (4 grams) sugar

1 tablespoon plus 1 teaspoon (25 grams) water

1 tablespoon (15 grams) extra-virgin olive oil or unsalted butter

FILLING AND FINISHING

1 cup (250 grams) ricotta

¼ cup (50 grams) sugar

1 large egg

1 egg yolk

5 to 6 threads saffron, crumbled

Finely grated zest of ½ lemon

Confectioners' sugar for dusting

FOR the dough, place all the ingredients in the bowl of a stand mixer fitted with the dough hook. Process on low speed until combined. Remove the dough from the bowl, knead by hand a few times, shape into a ball, and wrap with plastic wrap. Refrigerate for 30 minutes.

ROLL the refrigerated dough to a ¼-inch (⅔-centimeter) thickness. Cut out disks that are 4 inches (10 centimeters) in diameter. Transfer the disks to a parchment paper–lined baking sheet or jelly-roll pan and refrigerate until ready to fill.

PREHEAT the oven to 350°F.

FOR the filling, force the ricotta through a sieve to make it perfectly smooth. Mix the ricotta together with the sugar, egg, egg yolk, saffron, and lemon zest.

USING a regular table spoon, such as a soup spoon, place 2 spoonfuls (about 20 grams) of filling in the center of each disk of dough. Carefully place one disk in the center of your palm. Cup your palm to form the disk into a small cup without a lid. Crimp the edges of the dough all around. Transfer back to the parchment paper–lined pan and repeat with the remaining disks and filling. Bake until the filling browns, about 20 minutes. Cool to room temperature and dust with confectioners' sugar before serving.

DOLCI REGIONALI DI NATALE

You've probably noticed that for almost every occasion, every region of Italy has its own specialty. While panettone and pandoro are regional Christmas treats that are now eaten widely in the whole country, there are many other local delicacies that are prepared only in their areas of origin. Below are just a few of Italy's many regional Christmas desserts.

BUCCELLATO Sicilia's buccellato is a decoratively crimped pastry ring with a dried fig filling. Buccellati are small cookies with the same type of filling.

CALCIONETTI FRITTI Abruzzo celebrates the holiday with fried turnovers with a sweet chickpea filling.

CALZONCELLI These fried ravioli from Basilicata go by numerous names. The filling of chestnuts and chocolate is flavored with spices. Molise's calciuni are similar.

GUBANA Gubana is enjoyed in Friuli-Venezia Giulia for both Christmas and Easter. It is made by rolling a yeasted dough around a walnut filling, then rolling up the dough into a cylinder and setting it in a pan in the shape of a ring or spiral.

PETTOLE Pettole from Puglia are yeasted fritters served piping hot.

PINOCCATE These small sugar and pine nut confections from Umbria come in two versions: white or black with cocoa powder. Both are cut into diamond shapes.

ROCCOCÒ In addition to struffoli (opposite), Campania features crunchy baked almond rings with a peppery spice mix.

TORCIGLIONE Umbria's almond torciglione is shaped to resemble a serpent (or, according to some, an eel from one of the landlocked region's many lakes) with little triangular slits for scales.

TRONCHETTO DI NATALE Festive Yule log cakes sit on the tables of Piemonte.

STRUFFOLI

GLAZED TOWER OF FRIED PASTRIES

Serves 6   *Campania*

Struffoli are fried bits of dough that are coated in honey syrup and piled on top of one another before being festively decorated with sprinkles and candied fruit—basically a mound of tiny donuts. They are served in Campania for Christmas. Though it can get a little messy, traditionally diners simply pluck off pieces by hand.

DOUGH

3⅓ cups (400 grams) unbleached all-purpose flour, plus more for work surface

⅔ cup (130 grams) sugar

3 large eggs

3 egg yolks

6 tablespoons (85 grams) unsalted butter, softened

¼ teaspoon salt

FRYING AND FINISHING

Olive oil for frying

1½ cups (510 grams) honey

⅔ cup (130 grams) sugar

⅔ cup (100 grams) sprinkles

2 tablespoons (30 grams) diced candied citron

3 to 4 (30 grams) candied orange slices, halved

COMBINE the 3⅓ cups (400 grams) flour and sugar and form into a well on the work surface. Add the eggs, yolks, butter, and salt to the center and gradually draw in flour from the sides of the well until you have a crumbly dough. Knead the dough until well combined, form it into a ball, and let it rest, covered, at room temperature for 2 hours.

LIGHTLY flour a work surface. Pull off small bits of the dough and roll them to form cylinders about the width of a piece of chalk. Cut these into lengths slightly larger than chickpeas.

LINE baking sheets or jelly-roll pans with paper towels and set aside. Fill a pot with high sides with 1 inch of olive oil and place over medium heat. When the oil is hot, fry the pieces of dough until golden, working in batches if necessary. Remove with a slotted spoon or skimmer and drain on the paper towels.

IN a saucepan large enough to hold the fried dough, combine the honey, sugar, and ¼ cup (60 milliliters) water and cook over low heat until it forms a dark golden syrup. Turn off the heat (but leave the pan on the burner) and add the dough to the syrup. Stir well to coat. Transfer the coated pieces of dough to a serving platter and by hand (you may have to let them sit for a moment until they're cool enough to touch) or with a wooden spoon shape them into a cone. Scatter on the sprinkles, candied citron, and orange slices. Serve at room temperature.

CARTELLATE

FRIED RIBBON PASTRIES WITH VIN COTTO

Makes 2 to 3 dozen pastries   *Puglia*

In Puglia, fried rosettes of pastry are dipped in rich vin cotto, or wine must reduction, for a Christmas treat. Be sure to allow the dough to rest so that it will be relaxed enough to roll thin. You can also roll the dough using a hand-crank pasta machine.

2¾ cups plus 2 table-spoons (300 grams) pastry flour

¼ cup (50 grams) olive oil

¼ cup plus 2 tablespoons (100 milliliters) white wine

Oil for frying

1 cup (250 milliliters) vin cotto

Sprinkles and/or ground cinnamon for finishing

COMBINE the flour, olive oil, and wine in the bowl of a stand mixer fitted with the paddle. Beat until combined. Shape the dough into a ball, wrap in plastic wrap, and allow to rest at room temperature for 30 minutes. Roll out the dough to less than 1/10 inch (1 millimeter). With a fluted pastry wheel, cut the dough into strips 6 inches (15 centimeters) long and a little more than ½ inch (1½ centimeters) wide. Roll a strip around your finger in a spiral and crimp it every ¾ inch (2 centimeters) to form a rosette.

LINE baking sheets or jelly-roll pans with paper towels and set aside. Fill a pot with high sides with several inches of oil for frying and place over medium heat. When the oil is hot, fry the dough rosettes until golden, working in batches if necessary. Remove with a slotted spoon or skimmer and drain on the paper towels.

PLACE the vin cotto in a saucepan and heat until warm. Dip a pastry in the warm vin cotto until coated all over, then hold over the pan for a moment to drain before transferring to a serving platter. Repeat with remaining pastries. Scatter on sprinkles and/or ground cinnamon and serve.

MONTE BIANCO

CHESTNUT MOUNTAIN

Serves 8   *Valle d'Aosta*

Creating the meringue base for this delicious dessert offers a good way to practice your piping skills. It may help you to trace a circle on the underside of the parchment paper to use as a guide. This northern favorite resembling a snow-capped mountain is always a crowd-pleaser. If you would like your chestnut puree to be arranged in thick strands, use a potato ricer, but you can also puree the chestnuts more finely through a sieve or a clean garlic press if you prefer.

MERINGUE

3 egg whites

½ cup (100 grams) granulated sugar

¾ cup plus 2 tablespoons (100 grams) confectioners' sugar, sifted

FILLING AND
FINISHING

2 cups plus 2 tablespoons (500 grams) heavy cream

¼ cup plus 3 tablespoons (50 grams) confectioners' sugar

1 cup (250 grams) Crema Pasticcera (page 88)

1 (17.63-ounce/500-gram) jar candied chestnuts in syrup

PREHEAT the oven to 160°F (70°C). Line two baking sheets or jelly-roll pans with parchment paper and set aside. Whip the egg whites and granulated sugar to stiff peaks. With a silicon spatula, gently fold in the confectioners' sugar, retaining as much air and volume as possible. Transfer the mixture to a pastry bag fitted with a number 4 plain tube and pipe a 7-inch (18-centimeter) diameter spiral on one prepared pan. Pipe any leftover meringue onto the other pan. (You will crumble these pieces later, so don't worry about their shape.) Bake until dry to the touch but not browned, about 4 hours for the base, less for smaller pieces. Cool on the pan.

TRANSFER the meringue base to a serving platter. Whip the heavy cream to soft peaks, then add the confectioners' sugar and whip to stiff peaks. Spread the crema pasticcera on the meringue base. Reserve a couple of chestnuts; force the rest through a potato ricer or a clean garlic press and let the crushed chestnuts fall onto the base, moving the potato ricer in a spiral from the outside inward so that the crushed chestnuts form a mound that is taller in the center. Spread or pipe the whipped cream on the peak to resemble snow. Crumble the remaining meringue and cut the reserved chestnuts into a small dice and use those to decorate the top of the mountain.

TORRONE MORBIDO

SOFT NOUGAT

Makes six 8 by 2-inch bars

Nougat can either be soft—as it is here—or crispy, so that it breaks into craggy shards when cut. If substituting almonds, use raw almonds with the skins on, but if you substitute another type of nut (pistachios are also popular) they should be skinned. Edible confectionery rice paper is available in "letter-size" sheets, which means that the rice paper sheets in the United States are slightly shorter than the ones in Europe. You can cut the paper to fit your pan, but try not to overlap it. You will taste the honey in the nougat, so pick a high-quality honey. Acacia is a good choice.

Cooking spray for pan

2 to 4 (8 × 11-inch/21 × 29.7-centimeter) sheets confectionery rice paper

2½ cups (500 grams) sugar

2 tablespoons plus 1 teaspoon (50 grams) light corn syrup

1⅓ cups (450 grams) honey

3 egg whites

3⅓ cups (500 grams) hazelnuts, toasted, skinned, and cooled (see page 24)

⅓ cup (25 grams) diced candied orange peel (page 103)

SPRAY the sides and bottom of an 8 × 12-inch (33 × 23-centimeter) baking sheet or jelly-roll pan with cooking spray and line the bottom with confectionery rice paper. Put the sugar, corn syrup, and 7 tablespoons (100 milliliters) water in a saucepan, place over medium heat, and cook, stirring and brushing down the sides of the pan with a wet pastry brush, until the sugar has dissolved. Increase the heat and bring the mixture to a boil, then cook until it reaches 300°F (150°C) on a candy thermometer. At the same time in a separate saucepan, heat the honey until it reaches 250°F (125°C).

IN a stand mixer, beat the egg whites to soft peaks. When the sugar and honey reach the desired temperatures, gradually pour the hot honey into the egg whites with the mixer still running. Repeat with the hot sugar syrup. Beat on high speed for an additional 5 minutes, then fold in the hazelnuts and orange peel.

POUR the hot mixture into the prepared pan and spread it into the corners with an offset spatula. (The mixture will be stiff.) Place confectionery rice paper on top of the mixture, top with parchment paper, and use a rolling pin to smooth the surface, then remove the parchment paper. Allow the torrone to set at room temperature for 8 hours. When it is firm, slide it on the rice paper onto a work surface and cut into bars.

PASTIERA NAPOLETANA

WHEAT BERRY AND RICOTTA PIE

Makes one 9-inch (23-centimeter) pie, about 10 servings   *Campania*

Pastiera Napoletana is a delicious lattice-topped pie from Napoli with a filling of ricotta, wheat berries, lemon zest, orange flower water, cinnamon, candied fruit, and eggs. The version of pastiera we know today seems to have been invented in a convent, but it most likely derives from an ancient recipe for a cake that was offered to the pagan gods to ensure the safe return of sailors from the sea. Legend has it that the ever-frowning Queen Maria Theresa of Austria actually cracked a rare smile after tasting it. Pastiera is closely associated with Easter and its delicate floral aroma and flavor are certainly suited to spring. Cooked wheat berries are sold in jars (labeled as *grano cotto*).

DOUGH

2 cups plus 1 tablespoon (250 grams) unbleached all-purpose flour

¾ cup plus 2 tablespoons (100 grams) confectioners' sugar

1 stick plus 1 tablespoon (125 grams) unsalted butter, cold, cut into cubes

1 large egg

1 egg yolk

Finely grated zest of 1 lemon

FOR THE DOUGH, combine the flour and sugar and place on a work surface (or in a bowl) and form a well. Place the butter in the well. Work in the butter until it forms large chunks. Add the egg and yolk and knead until smooth. Add the finely grated lemon zest and knead to combine. Use a bench scraper to collect all the dough. Shape it into two logs (or disks), one using about two-thirds of the dough and one about one-third, and wrap in plastic wrap. Refrigerate for at least 1 hour and up to 3 days. Bring to room temperature before rolling.

FOR THE FILLING, place the cooked wheat berries in a saucepan over medium heat with the butter, milk and lemon zest. Bring to a gentle boil and stir occasionally until the mixture becomes very thick and creamy like oatmeal, about 15 minutes. Remove from the heat and refrigerate until cooled.

IN a bowl beat 2 of the eggs, the yolks, ricotta, sugar, vanilla, cinnamon and orange blossom water until smooth and creamy. Refrigerate for at least 3 hours and up to 12 hours.

FILLING

1 (10-ounce/280-gram) jar *grano cotto* (cooked wheat berries)

2 tablespoons (30 grams) unsalted butter

1 cup (240 milliliters) milk

Finely grated zest of 1 lemon

3 large eggs

2 egg yolks

12 ounces (350 grams) ricotta

1²/₃ cups (320 grams) sugar

1 teaspoon (4 grams) pure vanilla extract

1 teaspoon (3 grams) ground cinnamon

1 teaspoon (5 grams) orange blossom water

1¹/₃ cups (100 grams) chopped candied orange peel (page 103)

Confectioners' sugar for dusting

WHEN you are ready to bake the pie, preheat the oven to 400°F (200°C). Grease a 9-inch (23-centimeter) springform pan and set aside. Fold the cooled wheat berry mixture into the rested ricotta mixture and stir in the chopped candied orange peel.

ROLL out two-thirds of the pastry and place it in the prepared pan to line the bottom and sides. Roll out the remaining dough and cut strips about 1 inch wide using a pastry cutter. Fill crust with the ricotta mixture, level the top, and use the dough strips to make a lattice. (See page 76.) Trim any overhang. Vigorously whisk the remaining egg to make an egg wash and gently brush the lattice strips. Bake until golden, about 1 hour.

ALLOW to cool completely on a rack before removing the outside ring of the pan. Dust with confectioners' sugar and serve.

DOLCI DI PASQUA

JUST AS PANETTONE IS A SYMBOL OF CHRISTMAS IN MODERN ITALY, the colomba, a cake baked in a special pan to resemble a dove and usually dotted with pearl sugar, is a symbol of Easter. Like panettone, colomba is rarely if ever made at home. Indeed, it was industrial bakers who invented the modern colomba in a bid to extend their panettone earnings to another season. Like pandoro, colomba is quite plain and lends itself well to being filled or paired with macerated berries or Zabaione (page 151).

VENETO'S FUGASSA (dialect for focaccia) is a lightly sweetened Easter bread that bakes into a golden dome. It requires several days of preparation and rises multiple times.

IN ADDITION TO PASTIERA (page 128), the Campania region offers casatiello dolce, also known as pigna di Pasqua, a cake made with natural yeast, lard, and a shot of liqueur and given a long, slow rise. It is doused with white glaze and usually decorated with colored sprinkles.

THOUGH THE CASSATA OF SICILIA IS NOW EATEN YEAR-ROUND, it originated as an Easter dessert. It is made by lining a flared mold with Pan di Spagna (page 42), or sponge cake, and filling it with a ricotta mixture. The entire cake, when unmolded, is then covered in marzipan and elaborately decorated. Cassata is an ancient dessert—it dates back to the year 998, and its name derives from the Arabic *quasat*, a word for a large round bowl. A completely different type of cassata is made in the town of Ragusa for Easter. This is a pastry crust crimped around a ricotta filling, similar to the pardulas of Sardegna (page 120). Sicilia also produces lamb-shaped cakes and almond-paste sculptures in the shape of lambs for the season.

EGGS ARE A SYMBOL OF REBIRTH and therefore naturally associated with Easter. In Trentino–Alto Adige, the corona pasquale, or Easter crown, is a braided bread shaped into a wreath and often decorated with painted eggs. A similar anise-flavored sweet bread is formed into a nest in Liguria and wrapped around an egg. Chocolate eggs are popular in Italy for Easter, especially among children. Often they are hollow and contain small toys inside. Puglia's scarcelle cookies are also decorated with hard-boiled eggs and come in a variety of shapes.

TORTA DI CIOCCOLATO E CARAMELLO

SALTED CHOCOLATE AND CARAMEL TART

Makes one 9-inch (23-centimeter) tart, 8 to 10 servings

Nothing says festive celebration like chocolate. This rich dessert is a fitting end to a New Year's Eve dinner. Use a high-quality chocolate in the ganache— it really makes the tart. The crust is made with a chocolate variation of Pasta Frolla (page 67).

DOUGH

1 stick (8 tablespoons/ 110 grams) unsalted butter, at room temperature

½ cup plus 1 tablespoon (70 grams) confectioners' sugar

1 egg yolk

1 teaspoon (4 grams) pure vanilla extract

1¼ cups (150 grams) unbleached all-purpose flour

¼ cup (25 grams) unsweetened cocoa powder

CARAMEL

2 cups (400 grams) sugar

¼ cup (85 grams) light corn syrup

¼ cup (60 grams) heavy cream

1 stick (8 tablespoons/ 110 grams) unsalted butter, cut into 8 pieces

2 tablespoons (30 grams) crème fraîche

FOR the dough, in the bowl of a stand mixer fitted with the paddle attachment, cream the butter and confectioners' sugar until combined, about 1 minute. Add the egg yolk and vanilla and beat until smooth. Sift in the flour and cocoa powder and beat on low speed until just combined. Scrape the dough onto a sheet of plastic wrap and form into a disk. Chill until firm, at least 1 hour and up to 3 days.

ON a lightly floured surface, roll the tart dough into a circle a little less than ¼ inch (6 to 7 millimeters) thick. Transfer the dough to a 9-inch (23-centimeter) fluted tart pan with a removable bottom and press it into the pan. Chill the tart shell in the refrigerator for 30 minutes.

PREHEAT the oven to 325°F (160°C). After the tart shell has chilled, remove it from the refrigerator and prick the shell all over with a fork. Bake the shell until the pastry looks dry and set, 20 to 25 minutes. Transfer it to a wire rack and let it cool.

FOR the caramel, place ½ cup (120 milliliters) water in a large saucepan. Add the sugar and corn syrup and cook over medium-high heat, swirling the pan occasionally, until the mixture turns a medium amber caramel (it should reach 340°F/170°C on a candy thermometer), about 10 minutes. Remove the pan from the heat and carefully and gradually whisk in the heavy cream, butter, and crème fraîche. Be careful as the mixture will bubble furiously! Stir until smooth. Pour the caramel

GANACHE

3½ ounces (100 grams) bittersweet chocolate, finely chopped

½ cup (120 grams) heavy cream

Fleur de sel for finishing

Cocoa nibs

into the tart shell and allow it to set at room temperature, then place it in the refrigerator to chill.

FOR the ganache, place the chocolate in a heatproof bowl. In a small saucepan, bring the cream to a boil. Pour the hot cream over the chocolate, allow it to stand for 2 minutes, and then stir the mixture with a rubber spatula until smooth. Pour the ganache over the caramel and refrigerate until set.

REMOVE the tart from the refrigerator 5 to 10 minutes before you plan to serve it. Remove the ring carefully and place the tart on a serving platter. Sprinkle with fleur de sel and cocoa nibs to taste and serve.

CIOCCOLATO

Chocolate makes everything better, doesn't it? Chocolate has been made in Italy's Piemonte region since the sixteenth century, when the royal family (the Savoys, who were based in Torino) became fans. There's even a thick, rich chocolate drink named for them: cioccolata di Savoia. At Eataly we sell a wide array of chocolate confections.

MILK CHOCOLATE is made, as the name indicates, with milk or milk powder. It tends to be light in color and has a sweet flavor.

SEMISWEET CHOCOLATE AND BITTERSWEET CHOCOLATE are sometimes grouped together as dark chocolate. Bittersweet chocolate is less sweet than semi-sweet chocolate. Many brands of chocolate now print a cacao percentage on the wrapper, which tells you what portion of the chocolate comes from cocoa beans. The higher the number, the more intense the chocolate taste (and the less sweet the chocolate will be, as most of the remainder of the chocolate consists of sugar).

UNSWEETENED CHOCOLATE is used for baking but is not very palatable eaten out of hand! It has a very high cacao percentage because of its low sugar content.

COCOA POWDER is made by grinding the solids that remain after cocoa butter has been extracted. Cocoa powder is available in two forms: natural and Dutch-processed or alkalized. Dutch-processed cocoa powder is less acidic, and some prefer its milder flavor, while others are fans of the acidic taste of natural cocoa powder. They're interchangeable in all the recipes in this book. (And if you're curious, they're almost always interchangeable, with one exception: for cakes that use baking soda as a leavener, reach for the natural cocoa powder, because the baking soda feeds off the acid present in natural cocoa powder to make the cake rise.)

WHITE CHOCOLATE is made of cocoa butter, milk, and sugar, but none of the chocolate solids or liquor found in other chocolates, which is why it is not brown.

DOLCI AL CUCCHIAIO

Looking for comfort?
Soft, creamy spoon sweets always deliver.

BONET

CHOCOLATE TERRINE

Serves 8   *Piemonte*

Bonet (sometimes spelled bunet) is a terrine that was served as part of fancy banquets in Piemonte as early as the thirteenth century. A couple of hundred years later, when chocolate traveled from the New World to Europe, chefs began to include cocoa powder in bunet, along with other complementary flavorings. Eventually, crumbled almond and hazelnut cookies found their way into the mix as well—sometimes loaf-shaped bunet is garnished with a line of whole amaretti running vertically down the center like a row of buttons.

1¼ cups plus 6 tablespoons (330 grams) sugar

½ teaspoon (5 grams) salt

3 large eggs

1⅔ cups (400 grams) whole milk

⅓ cup (40 grams) cocoa powder

1 espresso made in a stovetop coffeemaker

14 amaretti cookies (page 20 or store-bought)

PREHEAT Preheat the oven to 325°F (160°C). Bring 1 cup (240 milliliters) water to a boil, then set aside.

MAKE a caramel by heating a small saucepan until very hot. Add 1¼ cups (250 grams) sugar a little at a time, waiting for the previous addition to melt before adding the next one. When all the sugar is melted, add the salt. When the mixture has reached a rich brown color, add the hot water, turning your face away from the pan. (Be very careful, as a great deal of steam will escape when you add the water.)

DIVIDE the caramel among eight 4-ounce (120-milliliter) foil cups.

WHISK the eggs in a large heatproof bowl. Combine the milk and remaining 6 tablespoons (80 grams) sugar in a saucepan and bring to a boil. Just as it begins to boil, remove from the heat. Temper the eggs by whisking in a tablespoon or so at a time of the hot milk mixture. When all the milk has been added, whisk in the cocoa powder and the espresso. Finally, crumble 6 of the amaretti cookies and add the crumbs to the mixture.

DIVIDE the mixture among the caramel-lined foil cups. Fill a baking pan with hot water and set the foil cups in the baking pan so that the water comes about halfway up the sides. Cover with aluminum foil. Bake in the preheated oven until set but still soft, about 30 minutes.

TO serve, fill a pan with hot water and set the ramekins or foil cups in it for a few minutes. Invert an individual plate over one foil cup, then turn both the plate and the cup. Lift off the cup. Repeat with the remaining cups. Top each individual serving with one whole cookie.

LATTE IN PIEDI
CRÈME CARAMEL

Serves 8 to 10

Though this flan with its slick of slightly bitter caramel is known in most places by its French moniker, in Italy it is known as "milk standing up," or alternatively as latte alla portoghese, which means Portuguese milk. In other words, no one is certain where in Europe this creamy treat originated, but everyone agrees it tastes great. This can be baked in a ring pan, a decorative pudding mold, or even in a Bundt pan.

1¼ cups plus 2 table-spoons (270 grams) sugar

2 cups (500 milliliters) whole milk

4 large eggs

¼ cup plus 3 tablespoons (100 grams) heavy cream

PREHEAT the oven to 250°F (120°C).

FOR the caramel, combine ¾ cup (150 grams) of the sugar with ⅓ cup (80 milliliters) water in a small saucepan. Whisk until the sugar is dissolved, then place over medium heat and simmer briskly until dark and caramelized. Immediately pour into a 3- to 4-cup (¾- to 1-liter) mold.

COMBINE the milk and the remaining ½ cup plus 2 tablespoons (120 grams) sugar in a small saucepan and place over medium-low heat just until the milk begins to bubble. Remove from the heat. Whisk the eggs in a large bowl. Whisk in the warm milk in a thin stream (whisk vigorously to stop the eggs from cooking, but if lumps do form, force the mixture through a sieve to make it smooth). Whisk in the cream, then pour the mixture into the mold on top of the caramel.

ARRANGE the mold in a baking pan and add boiling water to come about halfway up the sides of the cups. Bake in the preheated oven until just set in the center, about 1 hour and 10 minutes. Remove mold to a rack to cool. (Use tongs to remove it from the pan of water.) While the pudding is still slightly warm, run a butter knife around the edge, invert a platter on top, and unmold the pudding with the caramel on top.

ALTRI DOLCI AL CUCCHIAIO

SPOON SWEETS These include puddings, mousses, and the like and are mostly dairy based—are very popular in Italy. In Italy home ovens are a relatively recent arrival—even refrigerators were not found in the majority of Italian homes until decades after World War II. Since puddings and creams are cooked on the stovetop, they have been a popular choice as home-cooked desserts for generations.

BUDINO Budino means pudding, and puddings come in a range of flavors in Italy, though chocolate and vanilla are perhaps the most common. A pudding is thickened with starch, usually cornstarch or flour.

COPPA OR BICCHIERINO A coppa (meaning cup) or bicchierino (little glass) is a catchall term for a composed dessert. It might consist of layers of pastry cream, whipped cream, and cooked fruit, or dollops of mascarpone and chestnut puree with crumbled amaretti on top, or ricotta mixed with diced candied fruit and layered with small cubes of Pan di Spagna (page42). The possibilities are endless.

CREMA Crema is a custard. The Crema Pasticcera on page 88 may be spooned into bowls and eaten as a simple dessert, perhaps sprinkled with some flaked almonds.

CREMOSO A cremoso is similar to a pudding. It may be set with gelatin.

DOLCE LATTE This mild-mannered dessert is made with ricotta, cream, condensed milk, and a little gelatin to firm it up.

RISOLATTE To make risolatte, or rice pudding, simmer short-grain rice in lightly sweetened milk to cover until soft and thick, perhaps with a split vanilla bean in the mix. Sprinkle with a little ground cinnamon just before serving.

SANGUINACCCIO DOLCE This rich dark chocolate pudding from Puglia includes an unusual ingredient: pig's blood.

SEMIFREDDO Semifreddo is a frozen mousse. See our master recipe for making all flavors of semifreddo on page 168 and our recipe for a semifreddo studded with nougat on page 170.

SPUMA Spuma means foam but is a classic mousse. Chocolate is a favorite flavor.

ZUPPA INGLESE Italy's "English soup" likely takes its name from an English trifle. It layers Pan di Spagna (page 42) brushed with Alchermes, a bright pink spice liqueur from Toscana, with Crema Pasticcera (page 88) that may be flavored in various ways.

PANNA COTTA CON "STREUSEL" ALLA MANDORLA

PANNA COTTA WITH ALMOND STREUSEL

Serves 6   *Piemonte*

Panna cotta translates as "cooked cream," and indeed this dessert is as simple as that. Panna cotta originated in Piemonte—though it is now enjoyed everywhere in Italy—and there it is often topped with the famed local hazelnuts to create contrast with the silky smooth texture. We've taken that idea and run with it by inventing a crunchy almond streusel, but panna cotta can also be topped with melted chocolate, berries, or cooked fruit, or reverse the order in this recipe and drizzle the caramel on top.

1¾ cups (155 grams) granulated sugar

½ teaspoon (3 grams) salt

½ cup (150 grams) whole milk

3⅓ cups (800 grams) heavy cream

6 sheets (12 grams) gelatin

1¼ cups (150 grams) unbleached all-purpose flour

1¼ cups (150 grams) confectioners' sugar

1½ cups (150 grams) almond flour

Pinch ground cinnamon

1 stick plus 2 tablespoons (150 grams) unsalted butter, softened

BRING 1 cup (240 milliliters) water to a boil, then set aside. Make a caramel by heating a small saucepan until very hot. Add 1 cup (200 grams) granulated sugar a little at a time, waiting for the previous addition to melt before adding the next one. When all the sugar is melted, add the ½ teaspoon salt. When the mixture has reached a rich brown color, add the hot water, turning your face away from the pan. (Be very careful, as a great deal of steam will escape when you add the water.) Divide the caramel among six heatproof glasses or ramekins.

IN a saucepan, combine the milk, cream, and the remaining ¾ cup sugar and scald without letting the mixture come to a boil. Add the gelatin to the warm milk mixture and stir to dissolve completely. Spoon the mixture over the caramel in the glasses or ramekins and allow to cool to room temperature.

WHEN the panna cotta is cool, cover each glass or ramekin with plastic wrap and refrigerate until cold, at least 4 hours.

WHEN you are ready to serve the panna cotta, preheat the oven to 325°F (160°C) or use a toaster oven. In a mixing bowl, combine the all-purpose flour, confectioners' sugar, almond flour, cinnamon, and a pinch of salt. Stir in the softened butter with a wooden spoon.

LINE a baking sheet with parchment paper. Use your fingers to pinch off small pieces of the butter and flour mixture and drop the pieces onto the prepared baking sheet. Bake in the preheated oven until crisp and golden, about 20 minutes.

ALLOW the streusel mixture to cool slightly, then sprinkle on top of the panna cotta and serve.

TIRAMISÙ CLASSICO
TRADITIONAL TIRAMISÙ

Serves 10

The perfect balance of coffee and sweetness, tiramisù appropriately translates to "pick-me-up." The decadent Italian dessert is traditionally made with ladyfingers dipped in espresso, layered with a rich creamy mixture, and finished with a generous sprinkling of cocoa powder. Culinary legend has it that tiramisù was invented in Treviso, a small city in the romantic region of Veneto. Today, the classic dolce is made across Italy in a variety of ways; almost everyone in Italy will tell you that their family makes the best tiramisù. (See page 146 for a few variations.) This benefits from being made in advance, so it's a great choice when you're feeding a crowd. Because the eggs are uncooked, seek out the freshest eggs you can find from a trusted source.

5 large eggs

2 cups (480 grams) heavy cream

¼ cup plus 1 tablespoon (60 grams) sugar

2 cups (450 grams) mascarpone

1 cup (240 milliliters) espresso, hot (made in a stovetop coffee maker)

1 (8.8-ounce/250-gram) package ladyfingers or Novara cookies

¼ cup (30 grams) cocoa powder

SEPARATE the eggs. Whip the cream to stiff peaks. In a large bowl, whisk the egg yolks with the sugar and mascarpone until pale yellow and smooth. Whip the egg whites to stiff peaks. Using a wooden spoon, gently fold the egg whites into the mascarpone mixture, and then gently fold in the whipped cream.

POUR the coffee into a wide bowl and quickly dunk each cookie into it. Arrange about half of the cookies so that they completely cover the base of a shallow (about 1½ inches/4 centimeters deep) 11 × 7-inch (28 × 18-centimeter) dish. With a spatula, spread about half of the mascarpone mixture over the cookies.

ARRANGE another layer of soaked cookies on top of the mascarpone mixture, then top with the remaining mascarpone mixture. Sift the cocoa powder all over the top.

COVER the dish with plastic wrap and refrigerate for at least 4 hours before serving.

COME PERSONALIZZARE IL TIRAMISÙ

AMONG THE GENIUS INVENTIONS OF ITALIANS—pasta, opera, the radio—surely tiramisù ranks near the top. It is the home cook's secret sweet weapon. Easy enough to whip up at a moment's notice (without turning on the oven), it actually improves with age. Or so we're told—we're never able to keep it around for very long. The variations on tiramisù are endless, so feel free to make the recipe your own.

The building blocks of tiramisù are espresso (the "pick-me-up" that gives the dessert its name), mascarpone (a creamy cheese), and eggs. Here are some variations and additions you can use to make the dessert your own:

- Replace the ladyfingers with rectangles of Pan di Spagna (page 42) or another type of absorbent cake or cookie. This is a great way to use up baked goods that are beginning to go stale.

- Mix a little nocino (walnut liqueur) or another liqueur that marries well with coffee with the espresso before dunking the cookies.

- Top with chocolate shavings rather than cocoa powder.

- Make a caramel and drizzle it in between the layers. (At Eataly in New York, we make a special American version of tiramisù with salted roasted peanuts and caramel.)

- Fold chopped chocolate or nuts into the mascarpone mixture, or sprinkle them on top of the finished dish.

BIANCOMANGIARE
SICILIAN ALMOND PUDDING

Serves 10   *Sicilia*

Almond milk may seem like a newfangled invention, but in Sicilia—where almonds grow in abundance—it has been around since the Middle Ages. Like many of Sicilia's excellent sweets, this one has its roots in monasteries and convents.

10 grams (3 to 4 sheets) gelatin

2 cups plus 2 tablespoons (500 grams) almond milk

¼ cup plus 3 tablespoons (85 grams) sugar

2 cups plus 2 tablespoons (500 grams) heavy cream

About ¼ cup (25 grams) crushed pistachios

SOAK the gelatin sheets in cold water until softened, 5 to 10 minutes. Remove the sheets from the water and squeeze gently to drain.

WARM ¼ cup (55 grams) of the almond milk in a medium saucepan over low heat until lukewarm. Remove the saucepan from the heat and gently stir the softened gelatin sheets into the warm almond milk to melt. Add the sugar and remaining 2 cups (445 grams) almond milk and stir until completely dissolved. Transfer the liquid to a bowl and allow to cool completely.

WHIP the heavy cream to soft peaks and fold the whipped cream into the cooled almond milk mixture with a spatula.

FILL ten individual glass bowls with the mixture and refrigerate until firm, about 2 hours. Garnish with crushed pistachios on top and serve.

BAVARESE AL CIOCCOLATO BIANCO

WHITE CHOCOLATE BAVAROIS

Serves 8 to 10

A bavarese is similar to a mousse but made with gelatin for a slightly firmer texture. You can transfer this into individual molds or one large mold, or simply serve it out of a bowl. A raspberry coulis—a sauce made by pureeing fresh raspberries and straining out the seeds—makes the perfect tart accompaniment. Sometimes at Eataly we chill this in heart-shaped molds and place a heart-shaped piece of Pan di Spagna (page 000) on top that serves as a base once the dessert is unmolded.

20 grams (6 to 8 sheets) gelatin

5 egg yolks

¼ cup plus 3 tablespoons (90 grams) sugar

1 cup (250 grams) whole milk

1½ pounds (700 grams) white chocolate, chopped

5 cups (1,175 grams) heavy cream

SOAK the gelatin in cold water until softened, 5 to 10 minutes. Remove the sheets from the water and squeeze gently to drain. Whip the egg yolks and sugar until the sugar is dissolved and the mixture is pale yellow. Place the milk in a medium saucepan and bring to a boil over medium heat. Whisk the egg and sugar mixture into the milk once it has begun to boil and continue to cook, whisking constantly, until the mixture reaches a temperature of 185°F (85°C). Once the correct temperature has been reached, remove from the heat, add the softened gelatin, mix well, then add the chocolate a little at a time and mix until thoroughly combined and smooth. Cover with plastic wrap and set aside to cool.

ONCE the white chocolate mixture has cooled, whip the cream to soft peaks and fold it into the cooled mixture, working very gently to preserve as much volume as possible. Transfer to a mold or bowl or individual molds or bowls and refrigerate until firm, about 2 hours.

RICOTTA E MASCARPONE

THOUGH WE REFER TO RICOTTA AS A CHEESE, technically it is a byproduct
of cheesemaking. Ricotta is created using the whey from the milk of cows, sheep,
and water buffalo. Soft and mild, it is made largely in southern Italy. Ricotta can be
aged into a hard grating cheese, but in its soft, mild form it is a wonderful addition
to desserts. Sicilians in particular have made an art form of crafting creamy sweets
out of ricotta. It is used as a filling in Cannoli Siciliani (page 93) as well as to make
cassata, and as a filling for pastries. Ricotta is also a core ingredient in Pastiera
Napoletana (page 128). But ricotta on its own with a few embellishments is a
wonderful spoon sweet. It marries particularly well with honey and figs, or fold in some
chocolate chips and confectioners' sugar, spoon into glasses, top with a sprinkling of
cocoa powder, and serve, perhaps with a few crisp cookies for contrast.

MASCARPONE IS A DOUBLE OR TRIPLE CREAM CHEESE FROM LOMBARDIA.
Soft and silky, it is an essential ingredient in tiramisù (page 145) and can be folded
together with whipped cream and served alongside pandoro and panettone, or spread
in between two layers of Pan di Spagna (page 42). For a simple mascarpone treat,
make a sugar syrup and slowly drizzle the hot syrup into a bowl while beating 2 to
4 egg yolks with a mixer or vigorously by hand. Beat until the yolk mixture is cool.
Place the mascarpone in a large bowl, stir to loosen, and then fold in the egg yolk
mixture a little at a time. Spoon into small bowls or glasses, top with berries or
chocolate shavings, and serve. Mascarpone goes well with all kinds of fruit, as well
as chocolate, coffee, and liqueurs.

ZABAIONE

MARSALA CUSTARD

Serves 6

Zabaione, sometimes spelled zabaglione, is a rich custard whisked over boiling water until slightly thickened and foamy. There are many different recipes for zabaione. This one is adapted from *The Science of Cooking and the Art of Eating Well* by Pellegrino Artusi, a classic Italian cookbook that was first published in 1891 and continues to sell well in Italy to this day. Artusi mentions that you can also incorporate a little rum for a "more spirited" version, and that a little ground cinnamon tastes nice. The traditional way to measure the Marsala for this dish is to use the eggshells as measuring cups. Be sure to whisk constantly to prevent the eggs from curdling.

8 large egg yolks, at room temperature

½ cup (100 grams) sugar

16 half-eggshells (about 2 cups/480 milliliters) dry Marsala

6 baby mint leaves

FILL a saucepan with about 4 inches (10 centimeters) water. (To be used as the bottom of your bain-marie; when you rest the bowl on the pan, you'll want about an inch of space between the bowl and the water.) Bring the water to a simmer.

PLACE the egg yolks and sugar in a heatproof bowl and rest on top of the pot of boiling water. Whisk until the mixture is thick and pale. Gradually whisk in the Marsala. (If you are using the half-eggshell method, add one half-eggshell at a time.) Continue whisking constantly over the simmering water until the mixture begins to bubble. Pour into individual glasses or cups, garnish with the mint leaves, and serve warm.

GELATO, SORBETTO, GRANITA E SEMIFREDDO

Ice cream is a time machine:
one lick and you're a child again.

AFFOGATO

ICE CREAM "DROWNED" IN COFFEE

Serves 1

You can top an affogato with lightly sweetened whipped cream or chocolate-covered espresso beans, but honestly, we're not sure why you'd want to tamper with perfection. We like to scoop the gelato in advance and store it in the freezer in pretty glass bowls. Then simply line up the bowls, pour the hot espresso over the gelato, and serve.

1 scoop vanilla or hazelnut gelato

¼ cup hot espresso made in a stovetop coffee maker or espresso machine

SCOOP the gelato into a serving bowl, glass, or coffee cup.

POUR the hot espresso over the gelato. Serve immediately.

GELATO VS. ICE CREAM: LA DIFFERENZA

You will commonly find the word gelato translated as ice cream, but there are actually differences between the two. Gelato has more milk than cream, while ice cream uses the inverse proportions, so gelato has less fat than ice cream. Ice cream is also whipped at a higher speed than gelato, incorporating more air, and it's processed for a longer period of time. (Your ice cream maker may have a gelato setting, which whips the base more slowly. If it does, definitely use it!) Ice cream is drier feeling when you taste it and has a stiffer, more solid texture. Ice cream is stored at a lower temperature, too. Even the way we scoop gelato is different—we mash it around in the container while scooping for that softer consistency. Ice cream rolls up into a ball when you scoop it. Finally, a gelateria makes all of its gelato fresh every morning, so gelato doesn't have as much of a chance to freeze as ice cream does. Because gelato has less fat (never more than 11 percent), it melts more slowly in your mouth, and you taste it differently, too. It coats your tongue gradually, while ice cream tends to collect at the back of your palate. You are more likely to get an "ice cream headache" from ice cream than gelato.

GELATO ALLA CREMA
VANILLA ICE CREAM

Makes about 2 pints gelato

This is your basic form of gelato, and every other flavor uses this same method with slight variations. The base should be cooked to reach 185°F (85°C). This ensures that the eggs are heated to a safe temperature, and most importantly that the sugar has dissolved and so will not give the end result a gritty mouth feel.

1 cup (250 grams) whole milk

½ cup plus 1 tablespoon (110 grams) sugar

1 vanilla bean

1 egg yolk

⅔ cup (160 grams) heavy cream

IN a small pan combine the milk, ½ cup (100 grams) of the sugar, and the vanilla bean and place over low heat. In a small bowl, beat the egg yolk with the remaining 1 tablespoon (10 grams) sugar. When the milk starts to simmer, vigorously whisk in the yolk mixture. Cook the base until it reaches 185°F (85°C) or until it just starts to bubble again. Remove from the heat. Remove the vanilla bean and add the cream. Let the mixture cool completely in the refrigerator, then process in an ice cream machine according to the manufacturer's instructions, using the gelato setting if you have one. Transfer to containers and freeze.

VARIANTI DEL GELATO

GELATO AL FIOR DI LATTE *Fior di Latte Gelato* Because fior di latte (literally "flower of milk") has no vanilla or other distractions, it tastes purely of delicious dairy. Use the highest-quality milk and cream you can find. Omit the egg yolk and the vanilla bean from the Gelato alla Crema recipe and simmer the milk and sugar until the sugar has dissolved completely. Process in the machine, transfer to containers, and freeze.

GELATO AL PISTACCHIO *Pistachio Gelato* Make Gelato alla Crema. After the mixture has cooled, stir in a 7-ounce (200-gram) jar of pistachio paste, or make your own by pulsing 2 cups (200 grams) pistachios in a food processor fitted with the metal blade until the nuts form a paste. Process in the machine, transfer to containers, and freeze.

GELATO AL CREMINO *Chocolate–Hazelnut Swirl Gelato* Follow the instructions for Gelato alla Crema and after processing in the machine swirl in (do not thoroughly combine) a 7-ounce (200-gram) jar of hazelnut paste or make your own by pulsing 1⅓ cups (200 grams) skinned hazelnuts in a food processor fitted with the metal blade until the nuts form a paste. Also swirl in ½ cup (150 grams) chocolate-hazelnut spread, transfer to containers, and freeze.

GELATO AL TIRAMISÙ *Tiramisù Gelato* Follow the instructions for Gelato alla Crema, and after cooling, combine the base with the cream and ¾ cup (160 grams) mascarpone and process in the machine according to the manufacturer's instructions. After processing, fold in a crumbled espresso-dipped ladyfinger. Transfer to containers and freeze.

GELATO ALLA RICOTTA DI PECORA *Sheep's Milk Ricotta Gelato* Drain ⅔ cup (150 grams) sheep's milk ricotta. Make the base as for Gelato alla Crema and stir in the ricotta and cream together. Process according to the manufacturer's instructions, then fold in about ¼ cup (45 grams) chocolate chips and 1 or 2 crumbled cannoli shells. Transfer to containers and freeze.

GELATO AL BERGAMOTTO *Bergamot Gelato* Before making the base, scald the milk in a saucepan, add 1 Earl Grey teabag, and steep for 5 minutes. Remove teabag, add sugar, and proceed with Gelato alla Crema recipe. Transfer to containers and freeze.

GELATO AI FICHI *Fig Gelato* Process 1 pound 9 ounces (700 grams) fresh figs, stemmed (skins on), and the juice of 1 lemon in a food processor fitted with a metal blade or with an immersion blender until smooth. Proceed with Gelato alla Crema recipe, omitting the egg yolk and using only ½ cup (100 grams) sugar. Stir in the fig puree, process, and transfer to containers and freeze. You can replace the figs with other fruit, such as peeled peaches, ripe strawberries, or pitted cherries, but you will likely need to adjust the sugar depending on how sweet the fruit is. Taste the mixture before freezing to assess sweetness, but remember that gelato will taste less sweet once frozen. Always puree fruit until very smooth.

Gelato alla Stracciatella

Stracciatella does not have chocolate chips, but is filled with small chocolate flakes.

1. Make Gelato al Fior di Latte (page 157). Be sure to simmer the milk and sugar until the sugar has dissolved completely.

2. By hand with a large chef's knife finely chop about 3½ ounces (100 grams) chocolate into fine flakes. (Pieces should vary in size.)

3. When the base has cooled completely, stir the chocolate into the base.

COME ORDINARE IL GELATO

ORDER GELATO THE ITALIAN WAY:

1. Determine which size cone or cup you would like: piccolo, medio, or grande.

2. Ask how many flavors you may order for that size cone or cup. (There may be a sign hanging in the gelateria that indicates the number of flavors.)

3. Give some thought to a proper combination: fruit with fruit, chocolate with hazelnut, coffee with stracciatella. Vanilla is the joker of gelato and matches with almost anything.

BISCOTTI AL GELATO

ICE CREAM SANDWICHES ON COOKIES

Makes 5 sandwiches

Spread ice cream between cookies for a portable treat that's perfect for a cookout. We find these caramel cookies match beautifully with the fig gelato on page 157, but experiment with various flavors to explore other combinations.

3 tablespoons plus 1 teaspoon (50 grams) heavy cream

1 cup plus 2 tablespoons (230 grams) packed brown sugar, plus more for work surface

2 tablespoons (35 grams) unsalted butter, softened

4½ cups (550 grams) unbleached all-purpose flour

1½ pints fig gelato or other gelato of your choosing

MAKE A DRY CARAMEL: Place the cream in a saucepan and heat until warm. Meanwhile, place a large pot over medium heat and 1 tablespoon at a time add 1 cup (180 grams) of the brown sugar to the pan, stirring and waiting for the sugar to melt between additions. Adjust heat to guard against burning. When all the sugar has been incorporated and melted, carefully pour in the hot cream and stir to combine. Stir in the softened butter. When the butter is combined, add the flour and stir until combined. Remove from the heat and when the dough is cool enough to handle, knead briefly until smooth and uniform. Transfer the dough to a bowl, cover, and refrigerate for 2 hours.

AFTER 2 hours, knead the dough briefly on a clean work surface. Form it into 2 round logs about 2¾ inches (7 centimeters) in diameter. Place the logs on a pan or platter, cover with plastic, and refrigerate for 30 minutes.

PREHEAT the oven to 350°F (180°C). Line two baking sheets or jelly-roll pans with parchment paper and set aside. Sprinkle the remaining 2 tablespoons (50 grams) brown sugar on the work surface. Remove the dough logs from the refrigerator, brush them with water, and then roll them in the brown sugar so that they are coated on all sides.

CUT the logs into ⅒-inch- (½-centimeter-) thick slices and arrange them on the prepared pans, leaving 1 inch (2½ centimeters) between them. Bake in the preheated oven until crisp, about 12 minutes. Cool the cookies on the pans on a rack.

TO make the sandwiches, allow the gelato to soften slightly at room temperature, about 10 minutes. Scoop some gelato and place on the flat side (bottom) of a cookie. Gently spread with an offset spatula. (If the gelato resists, try dipping the spatula blade in hot water then wiping it off.) Top with another cookie, flat side (bottom) against the gelato. Repeat with the remaining cookies and gelato. Wrap the sandwiches in wax paper and freeze until serving.

BOMBOLONI CON GELATO

ICE CREAM SANDWICHES IN ITALIAN DOUGHNUTS

Makes 6 sandwiches

A fluffy bun split and filled with a scoop or two of gelato is a real treat—and a popular breakfast option in Italy, especially in Sicilia. We play off that tradition with an even more decadent option, a donut filled with ice cream. At Eataly we fry bomboloni in rice oil because it has such a neutral taste and high smoke point. You can find rice oil in Asian grocery stores, or use any other type of neutral oil, such as canola oil, that will not add any flavor to the bomboloni. In other words, skip the olive oil. If you prefer cream-filled bomboloni, you can pipe the pastry cream on page 88 into these doughnuts instead while they are still warm.

3 tablespoons plus 1 teaspoon (50 grams) whole milk

2¼ teaspoons/1 envelope (10 grams) active dry yeast

2 cups (250 grams) unbleached bread flour

1 tablespoon plus 1 teaspoon (20 grams) sugar

1 large egg

1 tablespoon (20 grams) unsalted butter, softened

½ teaspoon (3 grams) salt

Neutral oil for frying

Confectioners' sugar for dusting

About 2 pints gelato of your choice

SCALD the milk until it is just warm, then dissolve the yeast in the milk and set aside until creamy, about 5 minutes. Combine the flour and sugar in the bowl of a stand mixer fitted with the dough hook. With the mixer running, add the milk and yeast mixture and the egg. Beat until the mixture comes together to form a dough. Add the softened butter and beat until the dough is shiny and smooth. Sprinkle in the salt and beat for 2 to 3 additional minutes.

TRANSFER the dough to a large bowl, cover tightly with plastic wrap, and allow to rise at room temperature until doubled in size, 1 to 2 hours.

DIVIDE the dough into six equal portions and shape each portion into a ball. Press down gently to flatten into disks, then place them on a board or plate with plenty of room between them, loosely cover (just rest a piece of plastic wrap on top of the balls), and let rise at room temperature until doubled and very puffy and extensible, about 1 hour.

LINE a sheet pan with paper towels, place a cooling rack on top, and set aside. Fill a pot with high sides with several inches of oil; clip a candy thermometer to the pot. Bring the oil in the pan to 350°F (180°C) and fry the donuts. Work in batches to keep from crowding the pan and keep an eye on the oil temperature, adjusting heat

as needed. Fry until golden and puffed, turning once, 3 to 5 minutes per side. When the bomboloni are finished, with a skimmer remove to the prepared rack to drain. Wait for the oil temperature to come back up and repeat with the remaining donuts.

WHEN the bomboloni are cool enough to handle (but still deliciously warm), dust with confectioners' sugar, split horizontally with a serrated knife, fill with gelato, and serve.

SORBETTO AL LIMONE

LEMON SORBET

Serves 6 to 8

Dairy-free sorbetto is lighter than gelato and a refreshing end to any meal. Sorbetto can also be made with other types of fruit. Try folding candied nuts or chopped candied orange peel (page 103) into the finished sorbet. Or use lemon sorbet to make sgroppino (page 167). Be sure to put a few small glasses in the freezer in advance.

3 lemons

½ cup (100 grams) sugar

PEEL the lemon zest in large strips. Juice the lemons and reserve the juice. In a saucepan, combine 1 cup (240 milliliters) water with the sugar and lemon zest. Cook and stir over medium heat until the sugar has dissolved. Set aside to cool completely, then remove and discard the lemon zest. Stir in the lemon juice. Transfer the mixture to a gelato maker and process according to the manufacturer's instructions. Freeze until firm, about 4 hours, before serving.

SORBETTO ALLA PESCA

PEACH SORBET

Serves 6 to 8

The peaches for this sorbet must be supremely juicy for best results. Slightly over-ripe fruit is better than peaches that have not reached their prime.

¼ cup plus 2 tablespoons (75 grams) sugar

¼ cup (60 milliliters) freshly squeezed lemon juice

8 ripe medium peaches, peeled, pitted, and sliced

IN a saucepan, combine 1 cup (240 milliliters) water with the sugar and lemon juice. Cook and stir over medium heat until the sugar has dissolved. Set aside to cool completely, then transfer to a blender.

ADD the sliced peaches to the blender and process until the mixture is perfectly smooth. Transfer the mixture to a gelato maker and process according to the manufacturer's instructions. Freeze until firm, about 4 hours, before serving.

GRANITA DI PROSECCO

PROSECCO GRANITA

Serves 6 to 8

You don't need an ice cream maker to make granita. Simply create a flavored simple syrup, pour into a baking pan, freeze, then scrape with a fork to break it up.

2 tablespoons (25 grams) sugar

1 cup (240 milliliters) water

3 mint leaves

1½ cups (360 milliliters) Prosecco, preferably Flor Prosecco NV, Veneto

1 pint (170 grams) blackberries

MAKE a simple syrup by melting the sugar and water together in a small saucepan over low heat. Stir until the sugar has completely dissolved. Remove the pan from the heat and add the mint leaves to infuse the syrup for 5 minutes. Strain the syrup through a sieve into a medium bowl (discard the mint leaves) and mix in the Prosecco.

POUR the syrup into a shallow baking pan and freeze. Every 30 minutes or so for 4 hours, remove the dish from the freezer and scrape the mixture with a fork until the ice has splintered. To serve, scoop into bowls and garnish with the blackberries.

GRANITA DI ANGURIA *Watermelon Granita* Purchase a seedless watermelon or buy the seeded variety and pick out the seeds yourself as you're chopping it into small pieces. You can also substitute honeydew, cantaloupe, and other types of melon, though we love the bright red color. In a blender or food processor fitted with the metal blade, puree a little lemon juice, chopped watermelon flesh, and a simple syrup until smooth. Freeze as above.

GRANITA DI LIMONE *Lemon Granita* You can use the Sorbetto al Limone mixture on page 165 to make granita. Simply freeze as above, scraping occasionally with a fork, until crystallized rather than processing in a gelato maker. You can also incorporate a dash of limoncello into the mixture.

GRATTACHECCA *Shaved Ice* In addition to granita, Italians cool off in the summer with grattachecca: shaved ice drizzled with syrup. Unlike granita, grattachecca is rarely made at home. Instead, during the hot summers in grattachecca's native Rome, vendors in dedicated kiosks (many of which have been serving grattachecca for a century or more) shave ice off of a large block and transfer it to a cup, then drizzle on syrup, which filters down through the ice. You can easily convert any granita recipe into grattachecca by crushing your own ice and pouring the cooled syrup over it.

SGROPPINO

Place 1 scoop of Sorbetto
al Limone (page 165) and 1
tablespoon of vodka per person in a cold metal bowl and
whisk until incorporated. (You
can choose your degree of
slushiness—we like the sorbet mixture to remain firm.)
Scoop this mixture in small
balls and drop into glasses.
Gently pour in enough
Prosecco (or moscato) to
cover, and serve immediately.

SEMIFREDDO: RICETTA MADRE

FROZEN MOUSSE MASTER RECIPE

Serves 8

Semifreddo is a great dish to make when you're having people over for dinner. It's prepared in advance, it looks pretty, and—unlike ice cream—it doesn't require any special equipment. Below are instructions for making one large semifreddo in a loaf pan that you can then slice. (To make sharp cuts, run your knife under hot water and dry it between slices.) You can also portion the semifreddo into individual ramekins or bowls and either serve them as is or unmold them, or you can scoop it like ice cream if you'd rather. For a lighter semifreddo, you can omit the yolks completely and use about six whipped egg whites, and for a richer dessert, omit the whites and use eight or more egg yolks. You honestly cannot go wrong.

2 cups (480 grams) heavy cream

1¼ cups (250 grams) sugar

4 large eggs, separated

LINE a loaf pan with plastic wrap, letting it hang over the side about 2 inches, and set aside.

WHIP the cream to soft peaks. Add ¼ cup (50 grams) sugar and whip to stiff peaks. Set aside.

COMBINE the egg yolks and remaining 1 cup (200 grams) sugar in a heatproof bowl or the top of a double boiler. Bring a pot of water to a boil, set the bowl with the egg yolks on top, and whisk the yolks constantly over simmering water until thick and pale, about 5 minutes. Set aside to cool. Keep the pot of water on the stove.

PLACE the egg whites in a clean heatproof bowl. Set the bowl over the boiling water and beat until fluffy and glossy, about 5 minutes.

WHEN both the egg yolks and the whites have cooled, with a rubber spatula, fold the egg yolk mixture into the egg whites, then fold in the whipped cream. (You can leave streaks in the mixture or fold until it is thoroughly combined.) Transfer to the pan, smooth the top with an offset spatula, fold the plastic over the top to cover, and freeze until firm, about 4 hours.

SEMIFREDDO IN TUTTI I GUSTI

Now for the fun part—flavoring your semifreddo. You can add just about anything at any stage of creation.

FLAVOR THE WHIPPED CREAM Flavor whipped cream with a teaspoon of liqueur or extract.

FLAVOR THE EGG YOLKS Include lemon juice with the yolks while making the custard, or stir finely grated lemon zest into the finished custard. You can also incorporate a little vanilla extract or liqueur or espresso. Or add chopped chocolate to the warm custard and then whisk it in once it melts.

MIX-INS Mix in chopped or pureed fruit, grated or chopped chocolate, crumbled cookies, or chopped nuts. Swirl in a nut paste or chocolate spread or some jam for a marble effect. Or make layers of the mixture in the loaf pan with a thin layer of any of the above in between.

CRUST Add a layer of cookie crumbs on top of the semifreddo before freezing. When you overturn it, the crumbs will form a crust on the bottom.

SAUCE Serve slices in a pool of warm chocolate sauce or raspberry coulis.

SEMIFREDDO AL TORRONCINO
NOUGAT SEMIFREDDO

Serves 8

Torrone (page 127) can be chopped up and used as an ingredient in other dishes, and it makes a truly special semifreddo, fit for a special Christmas meal or any other occasion.

3 large egg yolks

⅓ cup (70 grams) sugar

1¼ cups (300 grams) heavy cream

4½ ounces (130 grams) hard torrone nougat

3½ ounces (100 grams) gianduia chocolate, chopped

LINE a loaf pan with plastic wrap, letting the plastic hang over the sides about 2 inches. Place the egg yolks in a heatproof bowl and set aside.

COMBINE the sugar with ⅓ cup (80 milliliters) water water in a saucepan. Bring to a boil, then pour over the egg yolks and whisk energetically until the mixture is cool.

IN a separate bowl, whip ¾ cup (180 milliliters) cream to soft peaks. Chop the nougat into crumbs.

FOLD the whipped cream and the chopped nougat into the egg yolk mixture.

TRANSFER the mixture to the prepared loaf pan and smooth the top with an offset spatula, taking care not to deflate the mixture.

FOLD the plastic wrap over the top to cover and freeze until firm, at least 8 hours. (Semifreddo can be made up to 3 days in advance.)

TO serve, scald the remaining ½ cup (120 milliliters) cream, and then whisk in the chopped gianduia. Place about 1 tablespoon of this sauce on each of eight individual serving plates.

TO slice the semifreddo, fold the plastic wrap back from the top. Invert a platter on top, then flip the loaf pan and platter together. Pull off the loaf pan, then gently peel off the plastic wrap. Cut the semifreddo into eight slices. Place one slice on each of the serving plates and serve immediately.

INDEX

First published in the United States of America in 2019 by
Rizzoli International Publications, Inc.
300 Park Avenue South New York, NY 10010
www.rizzoliusa.com

Copyright © 2019 Eataly, Inc.

Text: Natalie Danford
Photography: Francesco Sapienza, FrancescoSapienza.com
Prop Stylist: Maeve Sheridan
Publisher: Charles Miers
Editor: Tricia Levi
Design: Vertigo Design NYC
Production Manager: Barbara Sadick
Editorial Coordination: Jono Jarrett, Sarah Dowling
Managing Editor: Lynn Scrabis
Proofreader: Sarah Scheffel

Printed in China

2019 2020 2021 2022 / 10 9 8 7 6 5 4 3 2 1

ISBN: 978-0-8478-6496-6
Library of Congress Control Number: 2019942332

Visit us online:
Facebook.com/RizzoliNewYork
Twitter: @Rizzoli_Books
Instagram.com/RizzoliBooks
Pinterest.com/RizzoliBooks
Youtube.com/user/RizzoliNY
Issuu.com/Rizzoli

Born in Torino, Piemonte, Katia Delogu is the head pastry chef of Eataly North America.
For twenty years, she worked in various pastry shops in the Torino area, including the very
first Eataly. She was appointed head pastry chef of Eataly USA in 2010 upon the opening
of the American flagship store in New York City and has since overseen the opening of
stores in Chicago, Boston, Los Angeles, Las Vegas, and Toronto. She loves to share the
rich culinary history of her hometown and has written dozens of recipes inspired by
Italian tradition, including the recipe for Eataly's signature Tiramisù della Nonna.